3rd Wordplay: When Language Meets Games Workshop (Wordplay 2022)

Online
14 July 2022

ISBN: 978-1-7138-5647-4

Printed from e-media with permission by:

Curran Associates, Inc.
57 Morehouse Lane
Red Hook, NY 12571

Some format issues inherent in the e-media version may also appear in this print version.

Association for Computational Linguistics
209 N. Eighth Street
Stroudsburg, Pennsylvania 18360

Phone: 1-570-476-8006
Fax: 1-570-476-0860

acl@aclweb.org

Additional copies of this publication are available from:

Curran Associates, Inc.
57 Morehouse Lane
Red Hook, NY 12571 USA
Phone: 845-758-0400
Fax: 845-758-2633
Email: curran@proceedings.com
Web: www.proceedings.com

Wordplay 2022

The 3rd Wordplay: When Language Meets Games Workshop

Proceedings of the Workshop

July 14, 2022

Order copies of this and other ACL proceedings from:

Association for Computational Linguistics (ACL)
209 N. Eighth Street
Stroudsburg, PA 18360
USA
Tel: +1-570-476-8006
Fax: +1-570-476-0860
acl@aclweb.org

Introduction

The Wordplay workshop focuses on exploring the utility of interactive narratives, think everything from classic text-adventures like Zork to modern Twine games, to fill a role as the learning environments of choice for language-based tasks including but not limited to storytelling. A few previous iterations of this workshop took place very successfully with hundreds of attendees, at NeurIPS 2018 and NeurIPS 2020. Since then, the community of people working in this area has rapidly increased. This workshop aims to be a centralized place where all researchers involved across a breadth of fields can interact and learn from each other. Furthermore, it acts as a showcase to the wider NLP/RL/Game communities on interactive narrative's place as a learning environment. The program features a collection of invited talks in addition to contributed posters from each of these sections of the interactive narrative community and the wider NLP and RL communities.

For more information visit: `https://wordplay-workshop.github.io/`.

-The Wordplay's Organizing Committee

Organizing Committee

Organizing Committee

Prithviraj Ammanabrolu, Allen Institute for AI
Xingdi Yuan, Microsoft Research
Marc-Alexandre Côté, Microsoft Research
Ashutosh Adhikari, Microsoft Turing

Advisory Committee

Michiaki Tatsubori, IBM Research
Matthew Hausknecht, Argo AI
Kory Mathewson, DeepMind
Jack Urbanek, Meta AI Research
Adam Trischler, Microsoft Research
Jason Weston, Meta AI Research

Program Committee

Additional Reviewers

Guiliang Liu, University of Waterloo & Vector Institute
Raghuram Mandyam Annasamy, Google

Invited Speakers

Shrimai Prabhumoye, Nvidia
Tim Rocktäschel, University College London & Deepmind
Hal Daumé III, University of Maryland & Microsoft Research
Peter Jansen, University of Arizona
Lynn Cherny, GhostWeather

Keynote Talk: Controllable Text Generation for Interactive Virtual Environments

Shrimai Prabhumoye
Nvidia

Abstract: Since the dawn of the digital age, interactive virtual environments and electronic games have played a huge role in shaping our lives. Not only are they a source of entertainment but they also teach us important life skills such as strategic planning, collaboration, and problem solving. Therefore, online gamers expect their virtual environment to be aware of their situation (e.g., position in a game) and interact with them in natural language. In this talk, I describe novel techniques to generate text in a particular style. This talk provides an approach of generating engaging naturalistic conversation responses using knowledge generated by pre-trained language models, considering their recent success in a multitude of NLP tasks. The talk will conclude with exploring whether pretrained language models can be situated in these virtual spaces and generate dialogue in a zero-shot manner.

Bio: Shrimai Prabhumoye is a research scientist at Nvidia. She got her PhD degree in computer science from the Language Technologies Institute, Carnegie Mellon University. She was advised by Prof. Alan Black and Prof. Ruslan Salakhutdinov. She work on controllable text generation with focus on style, content and structure. She is also exploring the ethical considerations of controllable text generation. She co-designed the Computational Ethics for NLP course which was offered for the first time in Spring 2018 at CMU.

Keynote Talk: Knowledge Intensive Reinforcement Learning

Tim Rocktäschel
University College London & Deepmind

Abstract: Progress in Reinforcement Learning (RL) methods goes hand-in-hand with the development of challenging environments that test the limits of current approaches. While existing RL environments are either sufficiently complex or based on fast simulation, they are rarely both these things. Moreover, research in RL has predominantly focused on environments that can be approached tabula rasa, i.e., without agents requiring transfer of any domain or world knowledge outside of the simulated environment. I will talk about the NetHack Learning Environment (NLE), a scalable, procedurally generated, stochastic, rich, and challenging environment for research based on the popular single-player terminal-based rogue-like game, NetHack. We argue that NetHack is sufficiently complex to drive long-term research on problems such as exploration, planning, skill acquisition, and language-conditioned RL, while dramatically reducing the computational resources required to gather a large amount of experience. Interestingly, this game is extremely challenging even for human players who often need many years to solve it the first time and who generally consult external natural language knowledge sources like the NetHack Wiki to improve their skills. I will cover some of our recent work on utilizing language information in this challenging environment.

Bio: Tim Rocktäschel is a Researcher at DeepMind and an Associate Professor at the Centre for Artificial Intelligence at University College London (UCL). There, Tim is leading the UCL Deciding, Acting, and Reasoning with Knowledge (DARK) Lab. Tim is also a Scholar of the European Laboratory for Learning and Intelligent Systems (ELLIS). Before, he was a Manager, Research Scientist, and Area Lead at Meta AI (FAIR), a Postdoctoral Researcher in Reinforcement Learning at the Whiteson Research Lab at the University of Oxford, a Junior Research Fellow in Computer Science at Jesus College, and a Stipendiary Lecturer in Computer Science at Hertford College. Tim obtained his Ph.D. from UCL under the supervision of Sebastian Riedel, where he was awarded a Microsoft Research Ph.D. Scholarship in 2013 and a Google Ph.D. Fellowship in 2017. Tim's work focuses on Reinforcement Learning and Open-endedness.

Keynote Talk: Training Agents to Learn to Ask for Help in Virtual Environments

Hal Daumé III
University of Maryland & Microsoft Research

Abstract: Agent has largely become synonymous with autonomous agent, but I'll argue that scoping our study of agents to those that are fully autonomous is a mistake: instead, we should aim to train agents that can assist humans, and be assisted by humans. In line with this goal, I will describe recent and ongoing work in the space of assisted agent navigation, where agents can ask humans for help, and where they can describe their own behaviors. This talk will largely be based on joint work with Khanh Nguyen and Lingjun Zhao.

Bio: Hal Daumé III is a professor at University of Maryland, in the computer science department. He is also a Senior Principal Researcher at Microsoft Research NYC. Hal's main focuses are in natural language processing and machine learning; he studies questions related to how to get machines to becomes more adept at human language, by developing models and algorithms that allow them to learn from data. The two major questions that really drive their research these days are: (1) how can we get computers to learn through natural interaction with people/users? and (2) how can we do this in a way that minimize harms in the learned models?

Keynote Talk: ScienceWorld: Is your Agent Smarter than a 5th Grader?

Peter Jansen
University of Arizona

Abstract: Question answering models have rapidly increased their ability to answer natural language questions in recent years, due in large part to large pre-trained neural network models called Language Models. These language models have felled many benchmarks, including recently achieving an A grade on answering standardized multiple choice elementary science exams. But how much do these language models truly know about elementary science, and how robust is their knowledge? In this work, we present ScienceWorld, a new benchmark to test agents' scientific reasoning abilities. ScienceWorld is an interactive text game environment that tasks agents with performing 30 tasks drawn from the elementary science curriculum, like melting ice, building simple electrical circuits, using pollinators to help grow fruits, or understanding dominant versus recessive genetic traits. We show that current state-of-the-art language models that can easily answer elementary science questions, such as whether a metal fork is conductive or not, struggle when tasked to conduct an experiment to test this in a grounded, interactive environment, even with substantial training data. This presents the question of whether current models are simply retrieving answers to questions by way of observing a large number of similar input examples, or if they have learned to reason about concepts in a reusable manner. We hypothesize that agents need to be grounded in interactive environments to achieve such reasoning abilities. Our experiments provide empirical evidence supporting this hypothesis – showing that a 1.5 million parameter agent trained interactively for 100k steps outperforms an 11 billion parameter model statically trained for scientific question answering and reasoning via millions of expert demonstrations.

Bio: Peter Jansen is an Assistant Professor in the School of Information at the University of Arizona. A central focus of his research is how we can teach models to perform question answering while generating detailed human-readable explanations for their answers. His work is largely centered in the science domain, where he works to answer and explain standardized elementary and middle school science exams, as written, using a variety of automated inference formalisms. `http://www.cognitiveai.org/explanationbank/`

Keynote Talk: Text Toys and Glitch Poetics

Lynn Cherny
GhostWeather

Abstract: Not just a bug, the glitch offers creative possibility – especially in AI systems where we are travelers in a foggy latent space. The glitch is usually a visual metaphor, but it is alive and well in text encodings too. I'll talk about projects (mine and others') that explore neural spaces in poetic and game-like ways. Focusing on text play in this talk, we'll visit media collages, mistaken translations, cross-modal cutups, and the dusty bottoms of game databases in search of the uncanny glitch that make us laugh because it's true.

Bio: Lynn Cherny has a Ph.D. in linguistics from Stanford and worked in research on text-based virtual worlds (MUDs) and chat interfaces. She's been in industry as a UX desiger and data scientist for a hundred years now, at companies as diverse as Adobe, The Mathworks, TiVo, and Autodesk. She worked on the poetry generation algorithm for the UK Dubai 2020 pavilion and currently consults at Google Arts & Culture as an ML artist in residence, where she released a small game illustrated by AI-generated images. Lynn has given keynotes and talks on creative AI projects at Europython and PyData conferences, Eyeo Festival, and KIKK Festival. Her newsletter is a fun mashup of weird folklore, AI art, NLP, games & narrative links.

Table of Contents

A Systematic Survey of Text Worlds as Embodied Natural Language Environments

Peter A. Jansen
University of Arizona, Tucson, AZ
pajansen@arizona.edu

Abstract

Text Worlds are virtual environments for embodied agents that, unlike 2D or 3D environments, are rendered exclusively using textual descriptions. These environments offer an alternative to higher-fidelity 3D environments due to their low barrier to entry, providing the ability to study semantics, compositional inference, and other high-level tasks with rich action spaces while controlling for perceptual input. This systematic survey outlines recent developments in tooling, environments, and agent modeling for Text Worlds, while examining recent trends in knowledge graphs, common sense reasoning, transfer learning of Text World performance to higher-fidelity environments, as well as near-term development targets that, once achieved, make Text Worlds an attractive general research paradigm for natural language processing.

Zork
North of House You are facing the north side of a white house. There is no door here, and all the windows are barred. *>go north*
Forest This is a dimly lit forest, with large trees all around. One particularly large tree with some low branches stands here. *>climb large tree*
Up a Tree You are about 10 feet above the ground nestled among some large branches. On the branch is a small birds nest. In the bird's nest is a large egg encrusted with precious jewels, apparently scavenged somewhere by a childless songbird. *>take egg*
Taken. *>climb down tree*
Forest *>go north*

Table 1: An example Text World interactive fiction environment, Zork (Lebling et al., 1979), frequently used as a benchmark for agent performance. User-entered actions are *italicized.*

1 Introduction

Embodied agents offer an experimental paradigm to study the development and use of semantic representations for a variety of real-world tasks, from household tasks (Shridhar et al., 2020a) to navigation (Guss et al., 2019) to chemical synthesis (Tamari et al., 2021). While robotic agents are a primary vehicle for studying embodiment (e.g. Cangelosi and Schlesinger, 2015), robotic models are costly to construct, and experiments can be slow or difficult to scale. Virtual agents and embodied virtual environments help mitigate many of these issues, allowing large-scale simulations to be run in parallel orders of magnitude faster than real world environments (e.g. Deitke et al., 2020), while controlled virtual environments can be constructed for exploring specific tasks – though this benefit in speed comes at the cost of having to model virtual 3D environments, which can be substantial.

Text Worlds – embodied environments rendered linguistically through textual descriptions instead of graphically through pixels (see Table 1) – have emerged as a recent methodological focus that allow studying many embodied research questions while reducing some of the development costs associated with modeling complex and photorealistic 3D environments (e.g. Côté et al., 2018). More than simply reducing development costs, Text Worlds also offer paradigms to study developmental knowledge representation, embodied task learning, and transfer learning at a higher level than perceptually-grounded studies, enabling different research questions that explore these topics in isolation of the open problems of perceptual input, object segmentation, and object classification regularly studied in the vision community (e.g. He et al., 2016c; Szegedy et al., 2017; Zhai et al., 2021).

1.1 Motivation for this survey

Text Worlds are rapidly gaining momentum as a research methodology in the natural language processing community. In spite of this interest, many modeling, evaluation, tooling, and other barriers exist to applying these methodologies, with significant development efforts in the early stages of

Proceedings of the 3rd Wordplay: When Language Meets Games Workshop (Wordplay 2022), pages 1 - 15

mitigating those barriers, at least in part.

In this review, citation graphs of recent articles were iteratively crawled, identifying 108 articles relevant to Text Worlds and other embodied environments that include text as part of the simulation or task. Frequent motivations for choosing Text Worlds are highlighted in Section 2. Tooling and modeling paradigms (in the form of simulators, intermediate languages, and libraries) are surveyed in Section 3, with text environments and common benchmarks implemented with this tooling described in Section 4. Contemporary focuses in agent modeling, including coupling knowledge graphs, question answering, and common-sense reasoning with reinforcement learning, are identified in Section 5. Recent contributions to focus areas in world generation and hybrid text-3D environments are summarized in Section 6, while a distillation of near-term directions for reducing barriers to using Text Worlds more broadly as a research paradigm are presented in Section 7.

2 Why use Text Worlds?

For many tasks, Text Worlds can offer advantages over other embodied environment modelling paradigms – typically in reduced development costs, the ability to model large action spaces, and the ability to study embodied reasoning at a higher level than raw perceptual information.

Embodied Reasoning: Embodied agents have been proposed as a solution to the symbol grounding problem (Harnad, 1990), or the problem of how concepts acquire real-world meaning. Humans likely resolve symbol grounding at least partially by assigning semantics to concepts through perceptually-grounded mental simulations (Barsalou et al., 1999). Using embodied agents that take in perceptual data and perform actions in real or virtual environments offers an avenue for studying semantics and symbol grounding empirically (Cangelosi et al., 2010; Bisk et al., 2020; Tamari et al., 2020a,b). Text Worlds abstract some of the challenges in perceptual modeling, allowing agents to focus on higher-level semantics, while hybrid worlds that simultaneously render both text and 3D views (e.g. Shridhar et al., 2020b) help control what kind of knowledge is acquired, and better operationalize the study of symbol grounding.

Ease of Development: Constructing embodied virtual environments typically has steep development costs, but Text Worlds are typically easier to construct for many tasks. Creating new objects does not require the expensive process of creating new 3D models, or performing visual-percept-to-object-name segmentation or classification (since the scene is rendered linguistically). Similarly, a rich action semantics is possible, and comparatively easy to implement – while 3D environments typically have one or a small number of action commands (e.g. Kolve et al., 2017; Shridhar et al., 2020a), Text Worlds typically implement dozens of action verbs, and thousands of valid *Verb-NounPhrase* action combinations (Hausknecht et al., 2020).

Compositional Reasoning: Complex reasoning tasks typically require multi-step (or compositional) reasoning that integrates several pieces of knowledge in an action procedure that arrives at a solution. In the context of natural language, compositional reasoning is frequently studied through question answering tasks (e.g. Yang et al., 2018; Khot et al., 2020; Xie et al., 2020; Dalvi et al., 2021) or procedural knowledge prediction (e.g. Dalvi et al., 2018; Tandon et al., 2018; Dalvi et al., 2019). A contemporary challenge is that the number of valid compositional procedures is typically large compared to those that can be tractably annotated as gold, and as such automatically evaluating model performance becomes challenging (Jansen et al., 2021). In an embodied environment, an agent's actions have (generally) deterministic consequences for a given environment state, as actions are grounded in an underlying action language (e.g. McDermott et al., 1998) or linear logic (e.g. Martens, 2015). Embodied environments can offer a more formal semantics to study these reasoning tasks, where correctness of novel procedures could be evaluated directly.

Transfer Learning: Training a text-only agent for embodied tasks allows the agent to learn those tasks in a distilled form, at a high-level. This performance can then be transferred to more realistic 3D environments, where agents pretrained on text versions of the same environment learn to ground their high-level knowledge in low-level perceptual information, and complete tasks faster than when trained jointly (Shridhar et al., 2020b). This offers the possibility of creating simplified text worlds to pretrain agents for challenging 3D tasks that are currently out of reach of embodied agents.

3 Text World Simulators

Text World simulators render an agent's world view directly into textual descriptions of their environment, rather than into 2D or 3D graphical renderings. Similarly, actions the agent wishes to take are provided to the simulator as text (e.g. *"read the letter"* in *Zork*), requiring agent models to both parse input text from the environment, and generate output text to to interact with that environment.

In terms of simulators, the Z-machine (Infocom, 1989) is a low-level virtual machine originally designed by Infocom for creating portable interactive fiction novels (such as *Zork*). It was paired with a high-level LISP-like domain-specific language (ZIL) that included libraries for text parsing, and other tools for writing interactive fiction novels. The Z-machine standard was reverse-engineered by others (e.g. Nelson, 2014) in an effort to build their own high-level interactive fiction domain-specific languages, and has since become a standard compilation target due to the proliferation of existing tooling and legacy environments.[1]

Inform7 (Nelson, 2006) is a popular high-level language designed for interactive fiction novels that allows environment rules to be directly specified in a simplified natural language, substantially lowering the barrier to entry for creating text worlds. The text generation engine allows substantial variation in the way the environments are described, from dry formulaic text to more natural, varied, conversational descriptions. Inform7 is compiled to Inform6, an earlier object-oriented scripting language with C-like syntax, which itself is compiled to Z-machine code.

Ceptre (Martens, 2015) is a linear-logic simulation engine developed with the goal of specifying more generic tooling for operational logics than Inform 7. TextWorld (Côté et al., 2018) adapt Ceptre's linear logic state transitions for environment descriptions, and add tooling for generative environments, visualization, and RL agent coupling, all of which is compiled into Inform7 source code. Parallel to this, the Jericho environment (Hausknecht et al., 2020) allows inferring relevant vocabulary and template-based object interactions for Z-machine-based interactive fiction games, easing action selection for agents.

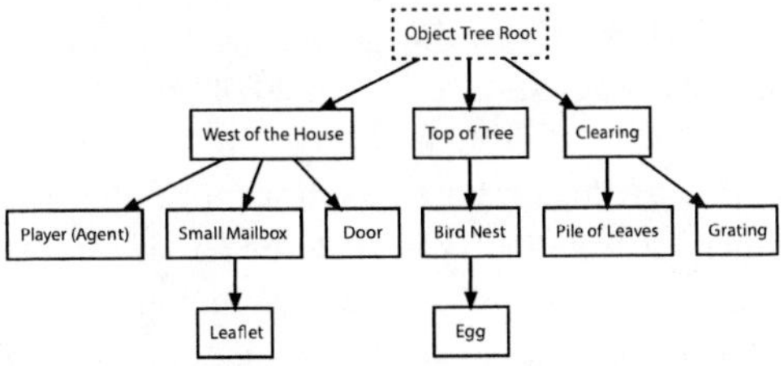

Figure 1: An example partial object tree from the interactive fiction game *Zork* (Lebling et al., 1979).

3.1 Text World Modeling Paradigms

3.1.1 Environment Modelling

Environments are typically modeled as an **object tree** that represents all the objects in an environment and their nested locations, as well as a set of **action rules** that implement changes to the objects in the environment based on an agent's actions.

Objects: Because of the body of existing interactive fiction environments for Z-machine environments, and nearly all popular tooling (Inform7, TextWorlds, etc.) ultimately compiling to Z-machine code, object models typically use the Z-machine model (Nelson, 2014). Z-machine objects have **names** (e.g. "mailbox"), **descriptions** (e.g. "a small wooden mailbox"), binary flags called **attributes** (e.g. "is_container_open"), and generic **properties** stored as key-value pairs. Objects are stored in the *object tree*, which represents the locations of all objects in the environment through parent-child relationships, as shown in Figure 1.

Action Rules: Action rules describe how objects change in response to a given world **state**, which is frequently a collection of preconditions followed by an action taken by an agent (e.g. *"eat the apple"*), but can also be due to environment states (e.g. a plant dying because it hasn't been watered for a time greater than some threshold). Ceptre (Martens, 2015) and TextWorld (Côté et al., 2018) use **linear logic** to represent possible valid **state transitions**. In linear logic, a set of *preconditions* in the state history of the world can be consumed by a rule to generate a set of *postconditions*, such as consuming a `closed(C)` precondition and posting a `open(C)` postcondition for a container-opening action for some container `C`.

Côté et al. (2018) note the limitations in existing implementations of state transition systems for text worlds (such as single-step forward or backward chaining), and suggest future systems may wish

[1]A variety of text adventure tooling, including the Adventure Game Toolkit (AGT) and Text Adventure Development System (TADS), was developed starting in the late 1980s, but these simulators have generally not been adopted by the NLP community in favour of the more popular Inform series tools.

to use mature **action languages** such as STRIPS (Fikes and Nilsson, 1971) or GDL (Genesereth et al., 2005; Thielscher, 2010, 2017) as the basis of a world model, though each of these languages have tradeoffs in features (such as object typing) and general expressivity (such as being primarily agent-action centered, rather than implementing environment-driven actions and processes) that make certain kinds of complex modeling more challenging. As a proof-of-concept, ALFWorld (Shridhar et al., 2020b) uses the Planning Domain Definition Language (PDDL, McDermott et al., 1998) to define the semantics for the variety of *pick-and-place* tasks in its text world rendering of the ALFRED benchmark.

3.1.2 Agent Modelling

While environments can be modelled as a collection of states and allowable state transitions (or rules), agents typically have incomplete or inaccurate information about the environment, and must make **observations** of the environment state through (potentially noisy or inadequate) sensors, and take **actions** based on those observations. Because of this, agents are typically modelled as partially-observable Markov decision processes (POMDP) (Kaelbling et al., 1998).

A Markov decision process (MDP) contains the state history (S), valid state transitions (T), available actions (A), and (for agent modeling) the expected immediate reward for taking each action (R). POMDPs extend this to account for partial observability by supplying a finite list of observations the agent can make (Ω), and an observation function (O) that returns what the agent actually observes from an observation, given the current world state. For example, the observation function might return *unknown* if the agent tries to examine the contents of a locked container before unlocking it, because the contents cannot yet be observed. Similarly, when observing the temperature of a cup of tea, the observation function might return coarse measurements *(e.g. hot, warm, cool)* if the agent uses their hand for measurement, or fine-grained measurements *(e.g.* $70°C$*)* if the agent uses a thermometer. A final discount factor (γ) influences whether the agent prefers immediate rewards, or eventual (distant) rewards. The POMDP defined by defined by $(S, T, A, R, \Omega, O, \gamma)$ then serves as a model for a learning framework, typically reinforcement learning (RL), to learn a policy that enables the agent to maximize the reward.

4 Text World Environments

Environments are worlds implemented in simulators, that agents explore to perform tasks. Environments can be simple or complex, evaluate task-specific or domain-general competencies, be static or generative, and have small or large action spaces compared to higher-fidelity simulators (see the Appendix for a comparison of action space sizes across environments and simulators).

4.1 Single Environment Benchmarks

Single environment benchmarks typically consist of small environments designed to test specific agent competencies, or larger interactive fiction environments that test broad agent competencies to navigate a large world and interact with the environment toward achieving some distant goal. Toy environments frequently evaluate an agent's ability to perform compositional reasoning tasks of increasing lengths, such as in the Kitchen Cleanup and related benchmarks (Murugesan et al., 2020b). Other toy worlds explore searching environments to locate specific objects (Yuan et al., 2018), or combining source materials to form new materials (Jiang et al., 2020). While collections of interactive fiction environments are used as benchmarks (see Section 4.3), individual environments frequently form single benchmarks. Zork (Lebling et al., 1979) and its subquests are medium-difficulty environments frequently used in this capacity, while Anchorhead (Gentry, 1998) is a challenging environment where state-of-the-art performance remains below 1%.

4.2 Domain-specific Environments

Domain-specific environments allow agents to learn highly specific competencies relevant to a single domain, like science or medicine, while typically involving more modeling depth than toy environments. Tamari et al. (2021) create a TextWorld environment for wet lab chemistry protocols, that describe detailed step-by-step instructions for replicating chemistry experiments. These text-based simulations can then be represented as *process execution graphs (PEG)*, which can then be run on real lab equipment. A similar environment exists for the materials science domain (Tamari et al., 2019).

4.3 Environment Collections as Benchmarks

To test the generality of agents, large collections of interactive fiction games (rather than single environments) are frequently used as benchmarks. While the Text-Based Adventure AI Shared Task initially evaluated on a single benchmark environment, later instances switched to evaluating on 20 varied environments to gauge generalization (Atkinson et al., 2019). Fulda et al. (2017a) created a list of 50 interactive fiction games to serve as a benchmark for agents to learn common-sense reasoning. Côté et al. (2018) further curate this list, replacing 20 games without scores to those more useful for RL agents. The Jericho benchmark (Hausknecht et al., 2020) includes 32 interactive fiction games that support Jericho's in-built methods for score and world-change detection, out of a total of 56 games known to support these features.

4.4 Generative Environments

A difficulty with statically-initialized environments is that because their structure is identical each time the simulation is run, rather than learning general skills, agents quickly overfit to a particular task and environment, and rarely generalize to unseen environments (Chaudhury et al., 2020). Procedurally generated environments help address this need by generating variations of environments centered around specific goal conditions.

The TextWorld simulator (Côté et al., 2018) allows specifying high-level parameters such as the number of rooms, objects, and winning conditions, then uses a random walk to procedurally generate environment maps in the Inform7 language meeting those specifications, using either forward or backward chaining during generation to verify tasks can be successfully completed in the random environment. As an example, the First TextWorld Problems shared task[2] used TextWorld to generate 5k variations of a cooking environment, divided into train, development, and test sets. Similarly, Murugesan et al. (2020a) introduce TextWorld CommonSense (TWC), a simple generative environment for household cleaning tasks, modelled as a *pick-and-place* task where agents must pick up common objects from the floor, and place them in their common household locations (such as placing *shoes* in a *shoe cabinet*). Other related environments include Coin Collector (Yuan et al., 2018), a generative environment for a navigation task, and Yin et al.'s (2019b) procedurally generated environment for cooking tasks.

Adhikari et al. (2020) generate a large set of recipe-based cooking games, where an agent must precisely follow a cooking recipe that requires collecting tools (e.g. *a knife*) and ingredients (e.g. *carrots*), and processing those ingredients correctly (e.g. *dice carrots, cook carrots*) in the correct order. Jain et al. (2020) propose a similar synthetic benchmark for multi-step compositional reasoning called SaladWorld. In the context of question answering, Yuan et al. (2019) procedurally generate a simple environment that requires an agent to search and investigate attributes of objects, such as verifying their existence, locations, or specific attributes (like edibility). On the balance, while tooling exists to generate simple procedural environments, when compared to classic interactive fiction games (such as *Zork*), the current state-of-the-art allows for generating only relatively simple environments with comparatively simple tasks and near-term goals than human-authored interactive fiction games.

5 Text World Agents

Recently a large number of agents have been proposed for Text World environments. This section briefly surveys common modeling methods, paradigms, and trends, with the performance of recent agents on common interactive fiction games (as categorized by the Jericho benchmark, Hausknecht et al., 2020) shown in Table 2.

Reinforcement Learning: While some agents rely on learning frameworks heavily coupled with heuristics (e.g., Kostka et al., 2017, Golovin), owing to the sampling benefits afforded by operating in a virtual environment, the predominant modeling paradigm for most contemporary text world agents is reinforcement learning. Narasimhan et al. (2015) demonstrate that "Deep-Q Networks" (DQN) (Mnih et al., 2015) developed for Atari games can be augmented with LSTMs for representation learning in Text Worlds, which outperform simpler methods using n-gram bag-of-words representations. He et al. (2016a, DRRN) extend this to build the Deep Reinforcement Relevance Network (DRRN), an architecture that uses separate embeddings for the state space and actions, to improve both training time and performance. Madotto et al. (2020) show that the Go-Explore algorithm (Ecoffet et al., 2019), which periodically returns to promising but underexplored areas of a world, can achieve higher scores than the DRRN with fewer steps. Zahvey et al. (2018, AE-DQN) use an Action Elimination Network (AEN) to remove sub-

[2] https://competitions.codalab.org/competitions/21557

Model	Detective (E)	Zork1 (M)	Zork3 (M)	OmniQuest (M)	Spirit (H)	Enchanter (H)
DRRN (He et al., 2016b)	0.55	0.09	0.07	0.20	0.05	0.00
BYU-Agent (Fulda et al., 2017a)	0.59	0.03	0.00	0.10	0.00	0.01
Golovin (Kostka et al., 2017)	0.20	0.04	0.10	0.15	0.00	0.01
AE-DQN (Zahavy et al., 2018)	–	0.05	–	–	–	–
NeuroAgent (Rajalingam and Samothrakis, 2019)	0.19	0.03	0.00	0.20	0.00	0.00
NAIL (Hausknecht et al., 2019)	0.38	0.03	0.26	–	0.00	0.00
CNN-DQN (Yin and May, 2019a)	–	0.11	–	–	–	–
IK-OMP (Tessler et al., 2019)	–	1.00	–	–	–	–
TDQN (Hausknecht et al., 2020)	0.47	0.03	0.00	0.34	0.02	0.00
KG-A2C (Ammanabrolu and Hausknecht, 2020)	0.58	0.10	0.01	0.06	0.03	0.01
SC (Jain et al., 2020)	–	0.10	–	–	0.0	–
CALM (N-gram) (Yao et al., 2020)	0.79	0.07	0.00	0.09	0.00	0.00
CALM (GPT-2) (Yao et al., 2020)	0.80	0.09	0.07	0.14	0.05	0.01
RC-DQN (Guo et al., 2020a)	0.81	0.11	0.40	0.20	0.05	0.02
MPRC-DQN (Guo et al., 2020a)	0.88	0.11	0.52	0.20	0.05	0.02
SHA-KG (Xu et al., 2020)	0.86	0.10	0.10	–	0.05	0.02
MC!Q*BERT (Ammanabrolu et al., 2020b)	0.92	0.12	–	–	0.00	–
INV-DY (Yao et al., 2021)	0.81	0.12	0.06	0.11	0.05	–

Table 2: Agent performance on benchmark interactive fiction environments. All performance values are normalized to maximum achievable scores in a given environment. Due to the lack of standard reporting practice, performance reflects values reported for agents, but is unable to hold other elements (such as number of training epochs, number of testing epochs, reporting average vs maximum performance) constant. Parentheses denote environment difficulty (E:Easy, M:Medium, H:Hard) as determined by the Jericho benchmark (Hausknecht et al., 2020).

optimal actions, showing improved performance over a DQN on *Zork*. Yao et al (2020, CALM) use a GPT-2 language model trained on human gameplay to reduce the space of possible input command sequences, and produce a shortlist of candidate actions for an RL agent to select from. Yao et al. (2021, INV-DY) demonstrate that semantic modeling is important, showing that models that either encode semantics through an inverse dynamic decoder, or discard semantics by replacing words with unique hashes, have different performance distributions in different environments. Taking a different approach, Tessler et al. (2019, IK-OMP) show that imitation learning combined with a compressed sensing framework can solve Zork when restricted to a vocabulary of 112 words extracted from walk-through examples.

Constructing Graphs: Augmenting reinforcement learning models to produce knowledge graphs of their beliefs can reduce training time and improve overall agent performance (Ammanabrolu and Riedl, 2019). Ammanabrolu et al. (2020, KG-A2C) demonstrate a method for training an RL agent that uses a knowledge graph to model its state-space, and use a template-based action space to achieve strong performance across a variety of interactive fiction benchmarks. Adhikari et al. (2020) demonstrate that a Graph Aided Transformer Agent (GATA) is able to learn implicit belief networks about its environment, improving agent performance in a cooking environment. Xu et al. (2020, SHA-KG) extend KG-A2C to use hierarchical RL to reason over subgraphs, showing substantially improved performance on a variety of benchmarks.

To support these modelling paradigms, Zelinka et al. (2019) introduce TextWorld KG, a dataset for learning the subtask of updating knowledge graphs based on text world descriptions in a cooking domain, and show their best ensemble model is able to achieve 70 F1 at this subtask. Similarly, Ammanabrolu et al. (2021a) introduce JerichoWorld, a similar dataset for world modeling using knowledge graphs but on a broader set of interactive fiction games, and subsequently introduce WorldFormer (Ammanabrolu and Riedl, 2021b), a multitask transformer model that performs well at both knowledge-graph prediction and next-action prediction tasks.

Question Answering: Agents can reframe Text World tasks as question answering tasks to gain relevant knowledge for action selection, with these agents providing current state-of-the-art performance across a variety of benchmarks. Guo et al. (2020b, MPRC-DQN) use multi-paragraph reading comprehension (MPRC) techniques to ask questions that populate action templates for agents, substantially reducing the number of training examples required for RL agents while achieving strong performance on the Jericho benchmark. Similarly, Ammanabrolu et al. (2020b, MC!Q*BERT) use contextually-relevant questions (such as *"Where am I?", "Why am I here?"*) to populate their knowledge base to support task completion.

Common-sense Reasoning: Agents arguably require a large background of common-sense or world knowledge to perform embodied reasoning in virtual environments. Fulda et al. (2017a) extract common-sense affordances from word vectors trained on Wikipedia using word2vec (Mikolov et al., 2013), and use this to increase performance on interactive fiction games, as well as (more generally) on robotic learning tasks (Fulda et al., 2017b). Murugesan et al. (2020b) combine the ConceptNet common-sense knowledge graph (Speer et al., 2017) with an RL agent that segments knowledge between general world knowledge, and specific beliefs about the current environment, demonstrating improved performance in a cooking environment. Similarly, Dambekodi et al. (2020) demonstrate that RL agents augmented with either COMET (Bosselut et al., 2019), a transformer trained on common-sense knowledge bases, or BERT (Devlin et al., 2019), which is hypothesized to contain common-sense knowledge, outperform agents without this knowledge on the interactive fiction game *9:05*. In the context of social reasoning, Ammanabrolu et al. (2021) create a fantasy-themed knowledge graph, ATOMIC-LIGHT, and show that an RL agent using this knowledge base performs well at the LIGHT social reasoning tasks.

6 Contemporary Focus Areas

World Generation: Generating detailed environments with complex tasks is labourious, while randomly generating environments currently provides limited task complexity and environment cohesiveness. World generation aims to support the generation of complex, coherent environments, either through better tooling for human authors (e.g. Temprado-Battad et al., 2019), or automated generation systems that may or may not have a human-in-the-loop. Fan et al. (2020) explore creating cohesive game worlds in the LIGHT environment using a variety of embedding models including Starspace (Wu et al., 2018a) and BERT (Devlin et al., 2019). Automatic evaluations show performance of between 36-47% in world building, defined as cohesively populating an environment with locations, objects, and characters. Similarly, human evaluation shows that users prefer Starspace-generated environments over those generated by a random baseline. In a more restricted domain, Ammanabrolu et al. (2019) show that two models, one Markov chain model, the other a generative language model (GPT-2), are capable of generating quests in a cooking environment, while there is a tradeoff between human ratings of quest creativity and coherence.

Ammanabrolu et al. (2020a) propose a large-scale end-to-end solution to world generation that automatically constructs interactive fiction environments based on a story (such as *Sherlock Holmes*) provided as input. Their system first builds a knowledge graph of the story by framing KG construction as a question answering task, using their model (AskBERT) to populate this graph. The system then uses either a rule-based baseline or a generative model (GPT-2) to generate textual descriptions of the world from this knowledge graph. User studies show that humans generally prefer these neural-generated worlds to the rule-generated worlds (measured in terms of interest, coherence, and genre-resemblance), but that neural-generated performance still substantially lags behind that of human-generated worlds.

Hybrid 3D-Text Environments: Hybrid simulators that can simultaneously render worlds both graphically (2D or 3D) as well as textually offer a mechanism to quickly learn high-level tasks without having to first solve grounding or perceptual learning challenges. The ALFWorld simulator (Shridhar et al., 2020b) combines the ALFRED 3D home environment (Shridhar et al., 2020a) with a simultaneous TextWorld interface to that same environment, and introduce the BUTLER agent, which shows increased task generalization on the 3D environment when first trained on the text world. Prior to ALFWorld, Jansen (2020) showed that a language model (GPT-2) was able to successfully generate detailed step-by-step textual descriptions of ALFRED task trajectories for up to 58% of unseen cases using task descriptions alone, without visual input. Building on this, Micheli (2021) confirmed GPT-2 also performs well on the text world rendering of ALFWorld, and is able to successfully complete goals in 95% of unseen cases. Taken together, these results show the promise of quickly learning complex tasks at a high-level in a text-only environment, then transferring this performance to agents grounded in more complex environments.

7 Contemporary Limitations and Challenges

Environment complexity is limited, and it's currently difficult to author complex worlds. Two competing needs are currently at odds: the desire for complex environments to learn complex skills, and the desire for environment variation to encourage robustness in models. Current tooling emphasizes creating varied procedural environments, but those environments have limited complexity, and require agents to complete straightforward tasks. Economically creating complex, interactive environments that simulate a significant fraction of real world interactions is still well beyond current simulators or libraries – but required for higher-fidelity interactive worlds that have multiple meaningful paths toward achieving task goals. Generating these environments semi-automatically (e.g. Ammanabrolu et al., 2020a) may offer a partial solution. Independent of tooling, libraries and other middleware offer near-term solutions to more complex environment modeling, much in the same way 3D game engines are regularly coupled with physics engine middleware to dramatically reduce the time required to implement forces, collisions, lighting, and other physics-based modeling. Currently, few analogs exist for text worlds. The addition of a *chemistry engine* that knows ice warmed above the freezing point will change to liquid water, or a *generator engine* that knows the sun is a source of sunlight during sunny days, or an *observation engine* that knows tools (like microscopes or thermometers) can change the observation model of a POMDP – may offer tractability in the form of modularization. Efforts using large-scale crowdsourcing to construct knowledge bases of commonsense knowledge (e.g., ATOMIC, Sap et al., 2019) may be required to support these efforts.

Current planning languages offer a partial solution for environment modelling. While simulators partially implement facilities for world modeling, some (e.g. Côté et al., 2018; Shridhar et al., 2020b) suggest using mature planning languages like STRIPS (Fikes and Nilsson, 1971) or PDDL (McDermott et al., 1998) for more full-featured modeling. This would not be without significant development effort – existing implementations of planning languages typically assume full-world observability (in conflict with POMDP modelling), and primarily agent-directed state-space changes, making complex world modeling with partial observability, and complex environment processes (such as plants that require water and light to survive, or a sun that rises and sets causing different items to be observable in day versus night) outside the space of being easily implemented with off-the-shelf solutions. In the near-term, it is likely that a domain-specific language specific to complex text world modeling would be required to address these needs while simultaneously reducing the time investment and barrier-to-entry for end users.

Analyses of environment complexity can inform agent design and evaluation. Text world articles frequently emphasize agent modeling contributions over environment, methodological, or analysis contributions – but these contributions are critical, especially in the early stages of this subfield. Agent performance in easy environments has increased incrementally, while medium-to-hard environments have seen comparatively modest improvements. Agent performance is typically reported as a distribution over a large number of environments, and the methodological groundwork required to understand when different models exceed others in time or performance over these environment distributions is critical to making forward progress. Transfer learning in the form of training on one set of environments and testing on others has become a standard feature of benchmarks (e.g. Hausknecht et al., 2020), but focused contributions that work to precisely characterize the limits of what can be learned from (for example) *OmniQuest* and transferred to *Zork*, and what capacities must be learned elsewhere, will help inform research programs in agent modeling and environment design.

Transfer learning between text world and 3D environments. Tasks learned at a high-level in text worlds help speed learning when those same models are transferred to more complex 3D environments (Shridhar et al., 2020b). This framing of transfer learning may resemble how humans can converse about plans for future actions in locations remote from those eventual actions (as when we apply knowledge learned in classrooms to the real world). As such, text-plus-3D environment rendering shows promise as a manner of controlling for different sources of complexity in multi-modal task learning (from high-level task-specific knowledge to low-level perceptual knowledge), and appears a promising research methodology for imparting complex task knowledge on agents that are able to navigate high-fidelity virtual environments.

References

Ashutosh Adhikari, Xingdi Yuan, Marc-Alexandre Côté, Mikuláš Zelinka, Marc-Antoine Rondeau, Romain Laroche, Pascal Poupart, Jian Tang, Adam Trischler, and Will Hamilton. 2020. Learning dynamic belief graphs to generalize on text-based games. *Advances in Neural Information Processing Systems*, 33.

Prithviraj Ammanabrolu, William Broniec, Alex Mueller, Jeremy Paul, and Mark Riedl. 2019. Toward automated quest generation in text-adventure games. In *Proceedings of the 4th Workshop on Computational Creativity in Language Generation*, pages 1–12.

Prithviraj Ammanabrolu, Wesley Cheung, Dan Tu, William Broniec, and Mark Riedl. 2020a. Bringing stories alive: Generating interactive fiction worlds. In *Proceedings of the AAAI Conference on Artificial Intelligence and Interactive Digital Entertainment*, volume 16, pages 3–9.

Prithviraj Ammanabrolu and Matthew Hausknecht. 2020. Graph constrained reinforcement learning for natural language action spaces. *arXiv preprint arXiv:2001.08837*.

Prithviraj Ammanabrolu and Mark Riedl. 2019. Playing text-adventure games with graph-based deep reinforcement learning. In *Proceedings of the 2019 Conference of the North American Chapter of the Association for Computational Linguistics: Human Language Technologies, Volume 1 (Long and Short Papers)*, pages 3557–3565, Minneapolis, Minnesota. Association for Computational Linguistics.

Prithviraj Ammanabrolu and Mark Riedl. 2021a. Modeling worlds in text. In *Thirty-fifth Conference on Neural Information Processing Systems Datasets and Benchmarks Track (Round 1)*.

Prithviraj Ammanabrolu and Mark O Riedl. 2021b. Learning knowledge graph-based world models of textual environments. *arXiv preprint arXiv:2106.09608*.

Prithviraj Ammanabrolu, Ethan Tien, Matthew Hausknecht, and Mark O Riedl. 2020b. How to avoid being eaten by a grue: Structured exploration strategies for textual worlds. *arXiv preprint arXiv:2006.07409*.

Prithviraj Ammanabrolu, Jack Urbanek, Margaret Li, Arthur Szlam, Tim Rocktäschel, and Jason Weston. 2021. How to motivate your dragon: Teaching goal-driven agents to speak and act in fantasy worlds. In *Proceedings of the 2021 Conference of the North American Chapter of the Association for Computational Linguistics: Human Language Technologies*, pages 807–833, Online. Association for Computational Linguistics.

Andrea Asperti, Carlo De Pieri, and Gianmaria Pedrini. 2017. Rogueinabox: an environment for roguelike learning. *International Journal of Computers*, 2.

Timothy Atkinson, Hendrik Baier, Tara Copplestone, Sam Devlin, and Jerry Swan. 2019. The text-based adventure ai competition. *IEEE Transactions on Games*, 11(3):260–266.

Chris Bamford. 2021. Griddly: A platform for ai research in games. *Software Impacts*, 8:100066.

Lawrence W Barsalou et al. 1999. Perceptual symbol systems. *Behavioral and brain sciences*, 22(4):577–660.

Yonatan Bisk, Ari Holtzman, Jesse Thomason, Jacob Andreas, Yoshua Bengio, Joyce Chai, Mirella Lapata, Angeliki Lazaridou, Jonathan May, Aleksandr Nisnevich, et al. 2020. Experience grounds language. In *Proceedings of the 2020 Conference on Empirical Methods in Natural Language Processing (EMNLP)*, pages 8718–8735.

Antoine Bosselut, Hannah Rashkin, Maarten Sap, Chaitanya Malaviya, Asli Celikyilmaz, and Yejin Choi. 2019. Comet: Commonsense transformers for automatic knowledge graph construction. In *Proceedings of the 57th Annual Meeting of the Association for Computational Linguistics*, pages 4762–4779.

Angelo Cangelosi, Giorgio Metta, Gerhard Sagerer, Stefano Nolfi, Chrystopher Nehaniv, Kerstin Fischer, Jun Tani, Tony Belpaeme, Giulio Sandini, Francesco Nori, et al. 2010. Integration of action and language knowledge: A roadmap for developmental robotics. *IEEE Transactions on Autonomous Mental Development*, 2(3):167–195.

Angelo Cangelosi and Matthew Schlesinger. 2015. *Developmental Robotics: From Babies to Robots*. The MIT Press.

Thomas Carta, Subhajit Chaudhury, Kartik Talamadupula, and Michiaki Tatsubori. 2020. Visualhints: A visual-lingual environment for multimodal reinforcement learning. *arXiv preprint arXiv:2010.13839*.

Subhajit Chaudhury, Daiki Kimura, Kartik Talamadupula, Michiaki Tatsubori, Asim Munawar, and Ryuki Tachibana. 2020. Bootstrapped Q-learning with context relevant observation pruning to generalize in text-based games. In *Proceedings of the 2020 Conference on Empirical Methods in Natural Language Processing (EMNLP)*, pages 3002–3008, Online. Association for Computational Linguistics.

Maxime Chevalier-Boisvert, Dzmitry Bahdanau, Salem Lahlou, Lucas Willems, Chitwan Saharia, Thien Huu Nguyen, and Yoshua Bengio. 2018. Babyai: A platform to study the sample efficiency of grounded language learning. *arXiv preprint arXiv:1810.08272*.

Marc-Alexandre Côté, Ákos Kádár, Xingdi Yuan, Ben Kybartas, Tavian Barnes, Emery Fine, James Moore, Matthew Hausknecht, Layla El Asri, Mahmoud Adada, et al. 2018. Textworld: A learning environment for text-based games. In *Workshop on Computer Games*, pages 41–75. Springer.

Bhavana Dalvi, Lifu Huang, Niket Tandon, Wen-tau Yih, and Peter Clark. 2018. Tracking state changes in procedural text: a challenge dataset and models for process paragraph comprehension. In *Proceedings of the 2018 Conference of the North American Chapter of the Association for Computational Linguistics: Human Language Technologies, Volume 1 (Long Papers)*, pages 1595–1604, New Orleans, Louisiana. Association for Computational Linguistics.

Bhavana Dalvi, Peter Jansen, Oyvind Tafjord, Zhengnan Xie, Hannah Smith, Leighanna Pipatanangkura, and Peter Clark. 2021. Explaining answers with entailment trees. *arXiv preprint arXiv:2104.08661*.

Bhavana Dalvi, Niket Tandon, Antoine Bosselut, Wentau Yih, and Peter Clark. 2019. Everything happens for a reason: Discovering the purpose of actions in procedural text. In *Proceedings of the 2019 Conference on Empirical Methods in Natural Language Processing and the 9th International Joint Conference on Natural Language Processing (EMNLP-IJCNLP)*, pages 4496–4505, Hong Kong, China. Association for Computational Linguistics.

Sahith Dambekodi, Spencer Frazier, Prithviraj Ammanabrolu, and Mark O Riedl. 2020. Playing text-based games with common sense. *arXiv preprint arXiv:2012.02757*.

Matt Deitke, Winson Han, Alvaro Herrasti, Aniruddha Kembhavi, Eric Kolve, Roozbeh Mottaghi, Jordi Salvador, Dustin Schwenk, Eli VanderBilt, Matthew Wallingford, Luca Weihs, Mark Yatskar, and Ali Farhadi. 2020. RoboTHOR: An Open Simulation-to-Real Embodied AI Platform. In *CVPR*.

Jacob Devlin, Ming-Wei Chang, Kenton Lee, and Kristina Toutanova. 2019. BERT: Pre-training of deep bidirectional transformers for language understanding. In *Proceedings of the 2019 Conference of the North American Chapter of the Association for Computational Linguistics: Human Language Technologies, Volume 1 (Long and Short Papers)*, pages 4171–4186, Minneapolis, Minnesota. Association for Computational Linguistics.

Adrien Ecoffet, Joost Huizinga, Joel Lehman, Kenneth O Stanley, and Jeff Clune. 2019. Go-explore: a new approach for hard-exploration problems. *arXiv preprint arXiv:1901.10995*.

Angela Fan, Jack Urbanek, Pratik Ringshia, Emily Dinan, Emma Qian, Siddharth Karamcheti, Shrimai Prabhumoye, Douwe Kiela, Tim Rocktaschel, Arthur Szlam, et al. 2020. Generating interactive worlds with text. In *Proceedings of the AAAI Conference on Artificial Intelligence*, volume 34, pages 1693–1700.

Richard E Fikes and Nils J Nilsson. 1971. Strips: A new approach to the application of theorem proving to problem solving. *Artificial intelligence*, 2(3-4):189–208.

Nancy Fulda, Daniel Ricks, Ben Murdoch, and David Wingate. 2017a. What can you do with a rock? affordance extraction via word embeddings. *arXiv preprint arXiv:1703.03429*.

Nancy Fulda, Nathan Tibbetts, Zachary Brown, and David Wingate. 2017b. Harvesting common-sense navigational knowledge for robotics from uncurated text corpora. In *Conference on Robot Learning*, pages 525–534. PMLR.

Michael Genesereth, Nathaniel Love, and Barney Pell. 2005. General game playing: Overview of the aaai competition. *AI magazine*, 26(2):62–62.

Michael S. Gentry. 1998. Anchorhead.

Jonathan Gray, Kavya Srinet, Yacine Jernite, Haonan Yu, Zhuoyuan Chen, Demi Guo, Siddharth Goyal, C Lawrence Zitnick, and Arthur Szlam. 2019. Craftassist: A framework for dialogue-enabled interactive agents. *arXiv preprint arXiv:1907.08584*.

Xiaoxiao Guo, Mo Yu, Yupeng Gao, Chuang Gan, Murray Campbell, and Shiyu Chang. 2020a. Interactive fiction game playing as multi-paragraph reading comprehension with reinforcement learning. In *Proceedings of the 2020 Conference on Empirical Methods in Natural Language Processing (EMNLP)*, pages 7755–7765.

Xiaoxiao Guo, Mo Yu, Yupeng Gao, Chuang Gan, Murray Campbell, and Shiyu Chang. 2020b. Interactive fiction game playing as multi-paragraph reading comprehension with reinforcement learning. In *Proceedings of the 2020 Conference on Empirical Methods in Natural Language Processing (EMNLP)*, pages 7755–7765, Online. Association for Computational Linguistics.

William H Guss, Brandon Houghton, Nicholay Topin, Phillip Wang, Cayden Codel, Manuela Veloso, and Ruslan Salakhutdinov. 2019. Minerl: A large-scale dataset of minecraft demonstrations. In *Proceedings of the Twenty-Eighth International Joint Conference on Artificial Intelligence*.

Stevan Harnad. 1990. The symbol grounding problem. *Physica D: Nonlinear Phenomena*, 42(1-3):335–346.

Matthew Hausknecht, Prithviraj Ammanabrolu, Marc-Alexandre Côté, and Xingdi Yuan. 2020. Interactive fiction games: A colossal adventure. In *Proceedings of the AAAI Conference on Artificial Intelligence*, volume 34, pages 7903–7910.

Matthew Hausknecht, Ricky Loynd, Greg Yang, Adith Swaminathan, and Jason D Williams. 2019. Nail: A general interactive fiction agent. *arXiv preprint arXiv:1902.04259*.

Ji He, Jianshu Chen, Xiaodong He, Jianfeng Gao, Lihong Li, Li Deng, and Mari Ostendorf. 2016a. Deep reinforcement learning with a natural language action space. In *Proceedings of the 54th Annual Meeting of the Association for Computational Linguistics*

(Volume 1: Long Papers), pages 1621–1630, Berlin, Germany. Association for Computational Linguistics.

Ji He, Mari Ostendorf, Xiaodong He, Jianshu Chen, Jianfeng Gao, Lihong Li, and Li Deng. 2016b. Deep reinforcement learning with a combinatorial action space for predicting popular Reddit threads. In *Proceedings of the 2016 Conference on Empirical Methods in Natural Language Processing*, pages 1838–1848, Austin, Texas. Association for Computational Linguistics.

Kaiming He, Xiangyu Zhang, Shaoqing Ren, and Jian Sun. 2016c. Deep residual learning for image recognition. In *Proceedings of the IEEE conference on computer vision and pattern recognition*, pages 770–778.

Infocom. 1989. Learning zil.

Vishal Jain, William Fedus, Hugo Larochelle, Doina Precup, and Marc G Bellemare. 2020. Algorithmic improvements for deep reinforcement learning applied to interactive fiction. In *Proceedings of the AAAI Conference on Artificial Intelligence*, volume 34, pages 4328–4336.

Peter Jansen. 2020. Visually-grounded planning without vision: Language models infer detailed plans from high-level instructions. In *Proceedings of the 2020 Conference on Empirical Methods in Natural Language Processing: Findings*, pages 4412–4417.

Peter Jansen, Kelly Smith, Dan Moreno, and Huitzilin Ortiz. 2021. On the challenges of evaluating compositional explanations in multi-hop inference: Relevance, completeness, and expert ratings. In *Proceedings of the 2021 Conference on Empirical Methods in Natural Language Processing (EMNLP)*.

Minqi Jiang, Jelena Luketina, Nantas Nardelli, Pasquale Minervini, Philip HS Torr, Shimon Whiteson, and Tim Rocktäschel. 2020. Wordcraft: An environment for benchmarking commonsense agents. *arXiv preprint arXiv:2007.09185*.

Matthew Johnson, Katja Hofmann, Tim Hutton, and David Bignell. 2016. The malmo platform for artificial intelligence experimentation. In *Proceedings of the Twenty-Fifth International Joint Conference on Artificial Intelligence*, pages 4246–4247.

Leslie Pack Kaelbling, Michael L Littman, and Anthony R Cassandra. 1998. Planning and acting in partially observable stochastic domains. *Artificial intelligence*, 101(1-2):99–134.

Tushar Khot, Peter Clark, Michal Guerquin, Peter Jansen, and Ashish Sabharwal. 2020. Qasc: A dataset for question answering via sentence composition. In *Proceedings of the AAAI Conference on Artificial Intelligence*, volume 34, pages 8082–8090.

Eric Kolve, Roozbeh Mottaghi, Winson Han, Eli VanderBilt, Luca Weihs, Alvaro Herrasti, Daniel Gordon, Yuke Zhu, Abhinav Gupta, and Ali Farhadi. 2017. Ai2-thor: An interactive 3d environment for visual ai. *arXiv preprint arXiv:1712.05474*.

Bartosz Kostka, Jaroslaw Kwiecieli, Jakub Kowalski, and Pawel Rychlikowski. 2017. Text-based adventures of the golovin ai agent. In *2017 IEEE Conference on Computational Intelligence and Games (CIG)*, pages 181–188. IEEE.

Heinrich Küttler, Nantas Nardelli, Alexander H Miller, Roberta Raileanu, Marco Selvatici, Edward Grefenstette, and Tim Rocktäschel. 2020. The nethack learning environment. *arXiv preprint arXiv:2006.13760*.

P David Lebling, Marc S Blank, and Timothy A Anderson. 1979. Zork: a computerized fantasy simulation game. *Computer*, 12(04):51–59.

Andrea Madotto, Mahdi Namazifar, Joost Huizinga, Piero Molino, Adrien Ecoffet, Huaixiu Zheng, Alexandros Papangelis, Dian Yu, Chandra Khatri, and Gokhan Tur. 2020. Exploration based language learning for text-based games. *arXiv preprint arXiv:2001.08868*.

Chris Martens. 2015. Ceptre: A language for modeling generative interactive systems. In *Proceedings of the AAAI Conference on Artificial Intelligence and Interactive Digital Entertainment*, volume 11.

Drew McDermott, Malik Ghallab, Adele Howe, Craig Knoblock, Ashwin Ram, Manuela Veloso, Daniel Weld, and David Wilkins. 1998. Pddl-the planning domain definition language.

Vincent Micheli and François Fleuret. 2021. Language models are few-shot butlers. *arXiv preprint arXiv:2104.07972*.

Tomas Mikolov, Ilya Sutskever, Kai Chen, Greg Corrado, and Jeffrey Dean. 2013. Distributed representations of words and phrases and their compositionality. *arXiv preprint arXiv:1310.4546*.

Volodymyr Mnih, Koray Kavukcuoglu, David Silver, Andrei A Rusu, Joel Veness, Marc G Bellemare, Alex Graves, Martin Riedmiller, Andreas K Fidjeland, Georg Ostrovski, et al. 2015. Human-level control through deep reinforcement learning. *nature*, 518(7540):529–533.

Keerthiram Murugesan, Mattia Atzeni, Pavan Kapanipathi, Pushkar Shukla, Sadhana Kumaravel, Gerald Tesauro, Kartik Talamadupula, Mrinmaya Sachan, and Murray Campbell. 2020a. Text-based rl agents with commonsense knowledge: New challenges, environments and baselines. *arXiv preprint arXiv:2010.03790*.

Keerthiram Murugesan, Mattia Atzeni, Pushkar Shukla, Mrinmaya Sachan, Pavan Kapanipathi, and Kartik Talamadupula. 2020b. Enhancing text-based reinforcement learning agents with commonsense knowledge. *arXiv preprint arXiv:2005.00811*.

Karthik Narasimhan, Tejas Kulkarni, and Regina Barzilay. 2015. Language understanding for text-based games using deep reinforcement learning. In *Proceedings of the 2015 Conference on Empirical Methods in Natural Language Processing*, pages 1–11, Lisbon, Portugal. Association for Computational Linguistics.

Graham Nelson. 2006. Natural language, semantic analysis, and interactive fiction. *IF Theory Reader*, 141:99–104.

Graham Nelson. 2014. The z-machine standards document version 1.1.

Vivan Raaj Rajalingam and Spyridon Samothrakis. 2019. Neuroevolution strategies for word embedding adaptation in text adventure games. In *2019 IEEE Conference on Games (CoG)*, pages 1–8. IEEE.

Maarten Sap, Ronan Le Bras, Emily Allaway, Chandra Bhagavatula, Nicholas Lourie, Hannah Rashkin, Brendan Roof, Noah A Smith, and Yejin Choi. 2019. Atomic: An atlas of machine commonsense for if-then reasoning. In *Proceedings of the AAAI Conference on Artificial Intelligence*, volume 33, pages 3027–3035.

Mohit Shridhar, Jesse Thomason, Daniel Gordon, Yonatan Bisk, Winson Han, Roozbeh Mottaghi, Luke Zettlemoyer, and Dieter Fox. 2020a. ALFRED: A Benchmark for Interpreting Grounded Instructions for Everyday Tasks. In *The IEEE Conference on Computer Vision and Pattern Recognition (CVPR)*.

Mohit Shridhar, Xingdi Yuan, Marc-Alexandre Côté, Yonatan Bisk, Adam Trischler, and Matthew Hausknecht. 2020b. Alfworld: Aligning text and embodied environments for interactive learning. *arXiv preprint arXiv:2010.03768*.

Robyn Speer, Joshua Chin, and Catherine Havasi. 2017. Conceptnet 5.5: An open multilingual graph of general knowledge. In *Proceedings of the AAAI Conference on Artificial Intelligence*, volume 31.

Christian Szegedy, Sergey Ioffe, Vincent Vanhoucke, and Alexander A Alemi. 2017. Inception-v4, inception-resnet and the impact of residual connections on learning. In *Thirty-first AAAI conference on artificial intelligence*.

Ronen Tamari, Fan Bai, Alan Ritter, and Gabriel Stanovsky. 2021. Process-level representation of scientific protocols with interactive annotation. In *Proceedings of the 16th Conference of the European Chapter of the Association for Computational Linguistics: Main Volume*, pages 2190–2202, Online. Association for Computational Linguistics.

Ronen Tamari, Chen Shani, Tom Hope, Miriam RL Petruck, Omri Abend, and Dafna Shahaf. 2020a. Language (re) modelling: Towards embodied language understanding. In *Proceedings of the 58th Annual Meeting of the Association for Computational Linguistics*, pages 6268–6281.

Ronen Tamari, Hiroyuki Shindo, Dafna Shahaf, and Yuji Matsumoto. 2019. Playing by the book: An interactive game approach for action graph extraction from text. In *Proceedings of the Workshop on Extracting Structured Knowledge from Scientific Publications*, pages 62–71.

Ronen Tamari, Gabriel Stanovsky, Dafna Shahaf, and Reut Tsarfaty. 2020b. Ecological semantics: Programming environments for situated language understanding. *arXiv preprint arXiv:2003.04567*.

Niket Tandon, Bhavana Dalvi, Joel Grus, Wen-tau Yih, Antoine Bosselut, and Peter Clark. 2018. Reasoning about actions and state changes by injecting commonsense knowledge. In *Proceedings of the 2018 Conference on Empirical Methods in Natural Language Processing*, pages 57–66, Brussels, Belgium. Association for Computational Linguistics.

Bryan Temprado-Battad, José-Luis Sierra, and Antonio Sarasa-Cabezuelo. 2019. An online authoring tool for interactive fiction. In *2019 23rd International Conference Information Visualisation (IV)*, pages 339–344. IEEE.

Chen Tessler, Tom Zahavy, Deborah Cohen, Daniel J Mankowitz, and Shie Mannor. 2019. Action assembly: Sparse imitation learning for text based games with combinatorial action spaces. *arXiv preprint arXiv:1905.09700*.

Michael Thielscher. 2010. A general game description language for incomplete information games. In *Proceedings of the AAAI Conference on Artificial Intelligence*, volume 24.

Michael Thielscher. 2017. Gdl-iii: a description language for epistemic general game playing. In *Proceedings of the 26th International Joint Conference on Artificial Intelligence*, pages 1276–1282.

Jack Urbanek, Angela Fan, Siddharth Karamcheti, Saachi Jain, Samuel Humeau, Emily Dinan, Tim Rocktäschel, Douwe Kiela, Arthur Szlam, and Jason Weston. 2019. Learning to speak and act in a fantasy text adventure game. In *Proceedings of the 2019 Conference on Empirical Methods in Natural Language Processing and the 9th International Joint Conference on Natural Language Processing (EMNLP-IJCNLP)*, pages 673–683.

Ledell Wu, Adam Fisch, Sumit Chopra, Keith Adams, Antoine Bordes, and Jason Weston. 2018a. Starspace: Embed all the things! In *Proceedings of the AAAI Conference on Artificial Intelligence*, volume 32.

Yi Wu, Yuxin Wu, Georgia Gkioxari, and Yuandong Tian. 2018b. Building generalizable agents with a realistic and rich 3d environment. *arXiv preprint arXiv:1801.02209*.

Zhengnan Xie, Sebastian Thiem, Jaycie Martin, Elizabeth Wainwright, Steven Marmorstein, and Peter

Jansen. 2020. WorldTree v2: A corpus of science-domain structured explanations and inference patterns supporting multi-hop inference. In *Proceedings of the 12th Language Resources and Evaluation Conference*, pages 5456–5473, Marseille, France. European Language Resources Association.

Yunqiu Xu, Meng Fang, Ling Chen, Yali Du, Joey Tianyi Zhou, and Chengqi Zhang. 2020. Deep reinforcement learning with stacked hierarchical attention for text-based games. *Advances in Neural Information Processing Systems*, 33.

Claudia Yan, Dipendra Misra, Andrew Bennnett, Aaron Walsman, Yonatan Bisk, and Yoav Artzi. 2018. Chalet: Cornell house agent learning environment. *arXiv preprint arXiv:1801.07357*.

Zhilin Yang, Peng Qi, Saizheng Zhang, Yoshua Bengio, William Cohen, Ruslan Salakhutdinov, and Christopher D. Manning. 2018. HotpotQA: A dataset for diverse, explainable multi-hop question answering. In *Proceedings of the 2018 Conference on Empirical Methods in Natural Language Processing*, pages 2369–2380, Brussels, Belgium. Association for Computational Linguistics.

Shunyu Yao, Karthik Narasimhan, and Matthew Hausknecht. 2021. Reading and acting while blindfolded: The need for semantics in text game agents. In *Proceedings of the 2021 Conference of the North American Chapter of the Association for Computational Linguistics: Human Language Technologies*, pages 3097–3102.

Shunyu Yao, Rohan Rao, Matthew Hausknecht, and Karthik Narasimhan. 2020. Keep CALM and explore: Language models for action generation in text-based games. In *Proceedings of the 2020 Conference on Empirical Methods in Natural Language Processing (EMNLP)*, pages 8736–8754, Online. Association for Computational Linguistics.

Xusen Yin and Jonathan May. 2019a. Comprehensible context-driven text game playing. In *2019 IEEE Conference on Games (CoG)*, pages 1–8. IEEE.

Xusen Yin and Jonathan May. 2019b. Learn how to cook a new recipe in a new house: Using map familiarization, curriculum learning, and bandit feedback to learn families of text-based adventure games. *arXiv preprint arXiv:1908.04777*.

Xingdi Yuan, Marc-Alexandre Côté, Jie Fu, Zhouhan Lin, Chris Pal, Yoshua Bengio, and Adam Trischler. 2019. Interactive language learning by question answering. In *Proceedings of the 2019 Conference on Empirical Methods in Natural Language Processing and the 9th International Joint Conference on Natural Language Processing (EMNLP-IJCNLP)*, pages 2796–2813, Hong Kong, China. Association for Computational Linguistics.

Xingdi Yuan, Marc-Alexandre Côté, Alessandro Sordoni, Romain Laroche, Remi Tachet des Combes, Matthew Hausknecht, and Adam Trischler. 2018. Counting to explore and generalize in text-based games. *arXiv preprint arXiv:1806.11525*.

Tom Zahavy, Matan Haroush, Nadav Merlis, Daniel J Mankowitz, and Shie Mannor. 2018. Learn what not to learn: Action elimination with deep reinforcement learning. *Advances in Neural Information Processing Systems*, 31:3562–3573.

Mikuláš Zelinka, Xingdi Yuan, Marc-Alexandre Côté, Romain Laroche, and Adam Trischler. 2019. Building dynamic knowledge graphs from text-based games. *arXiv preprint arXiv:1910.09532*.

Xiaohua Zhai, Alexander Kolesnikov, Neil Houlsby, and Lucas Beyer. 2021. Scaling vision transformers. *arXiv preprint arXiv:2106.04560*.

A Extended List of Simulators

Simulators provide the infrastructure to implement the environments, objects, characters, and interactions of a virtual world, typically through a combination of a scripting engine to define the behavior of objects and agents, with a rendering engine that provides a view of the world for a given agent or user. Simulators for embodied agents exist on a fidelity spectrum, from photorealistic 3D environments to worlds described exclusively with language, where a trade-off typically exists between richer rendering and richer action spaces. This fidelity spectrum (paired with example simulators) is shown in Table 3, and described briefly below. Note that many of these higher-fidelity simulators are largely out-of-scope when discussing Text Worlds, except as a means of contrast to text-only worlds, and in the limited context that these simulators make use of text.

3D Environment Simulators: 3D simulators provide the user with complex 3D environments, including near-photorealistic environments such as AI2-Thor (Kolve et al., 2017), and include physics engines that model forces, liquids, illumination, containment, and other object interactions. Because of their rendering fidelity, they offer the possibility of inexpensively training robotic models in virtual environments that can then be transferred to the real world (e.g. RoboThor, Deitke et al., 2020). Adding objects to 3D worlds can be expensive, as this requires 3D modelling expertise that teams may not have. Similarly, adding agent actions or object-object interactions through a scripting language can be expensive if those actions are outside what is easily implemented in the simulator (like creating *gasses*, or using a pencil or saw to *modify*

	3D Environment Simulators

–	AI2-Thor (Kolve et al., 2017)
–	CHALET (Yan et al., 2018)
–	House3D (Wu et al., 2018b)
–	RoboThor (Deitke et al., 2020)
D	ALFRED (Shridhar et al., 2020a)
D I	ALFWorld (Shridhar et al., 2020b)
	Voxel-Based Simulators

–	Malmo (Johnson et al., 2016)
–	MineRL (Guss et al., 2019)
	Gridworld Simulators
	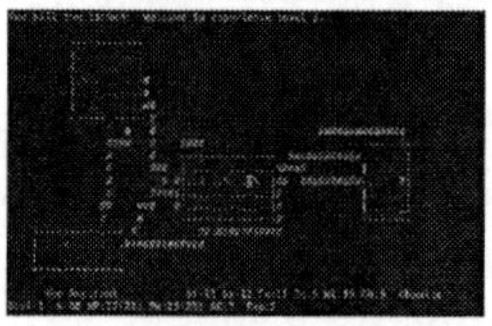
–	Rogue-in-a-box (Asperti et al., 2017)
D	BABYAI (Chevalier-Boisvert et al., 2018)
I	Nethack LE (Küttler et al., 2020)
I	VisualHints (Carta et al., 2020)
–	Griddly (Bamford, 2021)
	Text-based Simulators

I	Z-Machine (Infocom, 1989)
I	Inform7 (Nelson, 2006)
I	Ceptre (Martens, 2015)
I	TextWorld (Côté et al., 2018)
I	LIGHT (Urbanek et al., 2019)
I	Jericho (Hausknecht et al., 2020)

Table 3: Example embodied simulation environments broken down by environment rendering fidelity. **D** specifies that environments supply natural language *directives* to the agent, **I** specifies that environments are *interacted* with (at least in part) using natural language input and/or output, and no rating represents environments that do not have a significant text component.

Environment	# Actions	Examples
3D Environment Simulators		
ALFRED	7 Command	pickup, put, heat, cool
	5 Movement	move forward
Gridworld		
BABYAI	4 Command	pickup, drop, toggle
	3 Movement	turn left, move forward
NETHACK	77 Command	eat, open, kick, read
	16 Movement	move north, move east
Text-based		
ALFWorld	11 Command	goto, take, heat, clean
LIGHT	11 Command	get, drop, give, wear
	22 Emotive	applaud, wave, wink
PEG (Biomedical)	35 Command	incubate, mix, spin
Zork	56 Command	open, read, drop, drink

Table 4: Action space complexity for a selection of 3D, gridworld, and text-based environments.

an object). Because of this, action spaces tend to be small, and limited to movement, and one (or a small number of) interaction commands. Some simulators and environments include **text directives** for an agent to perform, such as an agent being asked to *"slice an apple then cool it"* in the ALFRED environment (Shridhar et al., 2020a). Other **hybrid environments** such as ALFWorld (Shridhar et al., 2020b) simultaneously render an environment both in 3D as well as in text, allowing agents to learn high-level task knowledge through text interactions, then ground these in environment-specific perceptual input though transfer learning.

Voxel-based Simulators: Voxel-based simulators create worlds from (typically) large 3D blocks, lowering rendering fidelity while greatly reducing the time and skill required to add new objects. Similarly, creating new agent-object or object-object interactions can be easier because they can generally be implemented in a coarser manner – though some kinds of basic spatial actions (like rotating an object in increments smaller than 90 degrees) are generally not easily implemented. Malmo (Johnson et al., 2016) and MineRL (Guss et al., 2019) offer wrappers and training data to build agents in the popular Minecraft environment. While the agent's action space is limited in Minecraft (see Table 4), the crafting nature of the game (that allows collecting, creating, destroying, or combining objects using one or more voxels) affords exploring a variety of compositional reasoning tasks with a low barrier to entry, while still using a 3D environment. Text directives, like those in CraftAssist (Gray et al., 2019), allow agents to learn to perform compositional crafting actions in this 3D environment from natural language dialog.

GridWorld Simulators: 2D gridworlds are comparatively easier to construct than 3D environments, and as such more options are available. GridWorlds share the commonality that they exist on a discretized 2D plane, typically containing a maximum of a few dozen cells on either dimension. Cells are discrete locations that (in the simplest case) contain up to a single agent or object, while more complex simulators allow cells to contain more than one object, including containers. Agents move on the plane through simplified spatial dynamics, at a minimum *rotate left, rotate right, and move forward*, allowing the entire world to be explored through a small action space.

Where gridworlds tend to differ is in their rendering fidelity, and their non-movement action spaces. In terms of rendering, some (such as BABYAI, Chevalier-Boisvert et al., 2018) render a world graphically, using pixels, with simplified shapes for improving rendering throughput and reducing RL agent training time. Others such as NetHack (Küttler et al., 2020) are rendered purely as textual characters, owing to their original nature as early terminal-only games. Some simulators (e.g. Griddly, Bamford, 2021) support a range of rendering fidelities, from sprites (slowest) to shapes to text characters (fastest), depending on how critical rendering fidelity is for experimentation. As with 3D simulators, hybrid environments (like VisualHints, Carta et al., 2020) exist, where environments are simultaneously rendered as a Text World and accompanying GridWorld that provides an explicit spatial map.

Action spaces vary considerably in GridWorld simulators (see Table 4), owing to the different scripting environments that each affords. Some environments have a small set of hardcoded environment rules (e.g. BABYAI), while others (e.g. NetHack) offer nearly 100 agent actions, rich crafting, and complex agent-object interactions. Text can occur in the form of task directives (e.g. *"put a ball next to the blue door"* in BABYAI), partial natural language descriptions of changes in the environmental state (e.g. *"You are being attacked by an orc"* in NetHack), or as full Text World descriptions in hybrid environments.

A Minimal Computational Improviser Based on Oral Thought

Nick Montfort
MIT Trope Tank
77 Mass Ave, 14E-316
Cambridge, MA 02139 USA
nickm@nickm.com

Sebastian Bartlett Fernandez
MIT Trope Tank
77 Mass Ave, 14E-316
Cambridge, MA 02139 USA
sebbb@mit.edu

Abstract

We describe our system for playing a minimal improvisational game in a group. In Chain Reaction, players collectively build a chain of word pairs or solid compounds. The game emphasizes memory and rapid improvisation, while absurdity and humor increases during play. Our approach is unique in that we have grounded our work in the principles of oral culture according to Walter Ong, an early scholar of orature. We show how a simple computer model can be designed to embody many aspects of oral poetics, suggesting design directions for other work in oral improvisation and poetics. The opportunities for our system's further development include creating culturally specific automated players; situating play in different temporal, physical, and social contexts; and constructing a more elaborate improvisor.

1 Introduction

We developed a prototype computer system to play the game Chain Reaction. This is both a memory game and an oral improvisational game, and may be the simplest such game. The game is best introduced with an example. Consider four players sitting in a circle, uttering the following:

- **Player 1,** beginning the game: Post office.
- **Player 2:** Post office chair.
- **Player 3:** Post office chair man [chairman].
- **Player 4:** Post office chair man child [manchild].
- **Player 1:** Post office chair man child labor.
- **Player 2:** Post office chair man child labor law.
- **Player 3:** Post office chair man child labor law school.
- **Player 4:** Post office chair man child labor law school boy [schoolboy].
- **Player 1:** Post office chair man child labor law school boy band.
- **Player 2:** Post office chair man child labor law school boy band ["banned"] book.
- **Player 3:** Post office chair man child labor law school boy banned book shelf [bookshelf].
- **Player 4:** Post office chair man child labor law school boy banned book shelf ... uh, I can't think of anything!
- **Player 2:** Shelf life!
- **Player 1:** Too late! Let's start again.

Each player's task is to continue the chain by reciting it quickly, without hesitation, and to immediately add a word that will create a coherent pair with the word before it. "Coherent" simply means that the pair must refer to a meaningful single item or concept. In written language we could call this a collocation or a bigram, but a pair could also form a solid compound such as "chairman" or "manchild." There is no requirement that the added word make any sense when joined together with any *earlier* words, only that the last word and the added word together constitute "a thing." As seen in the case of band/banned, words are considered to be oral units and it is fine to continue the chain while treating the previous word as a homophone. Typically, there is a prohibition on re-using words within the same game. Although this example doesn't show it, it's fine to use verb phrases (e.g., "slide off," "run up"), which also constitute "a thing." Many of these are easy to continue (e.g., "off brand," "up hill").

What exactly is "a thing"? Like obscenity, we know it when we see it, or in this case, when we hear it. "A thing" is determined by consensus. It is whatever the group accepts as a suitable two-word phrase or compound word. In the example given, Player 2 might have made a first move that involved uttering "post office plant" (an office plant being similar to a house plant, but for the office). This would have been a less obvious phrase, yet probably acceptable. Even so, the continuations "office salad" and "office sky" would probably not have been accepted, even if the player could have spun a story about how there are such things (a salad

Proceedings of the 3rd Wordplay: When Language Meets Games Workshop (Wordplay 2022), pages 16 - 24
July 14, 2022

stored in the office kitchen's fridge and consumed at one's desk or the view of the sky from one's office, for instance). If a player has to stop to explain the phrase, the game's continuity is broken, so such phrases are, at least, not *good* moves.

New players usually find it surprisingly easy to recite long chains. There are reasons for this related to oral practices. A fundamental reason involves shared cultural and linguistic expectations. Each word pair in the chain, after all, was almost instantly thought up by a player.

2 Why Build Computational Models of Oral Improvisation?

There has been intriguing work done to implement interactive improvisational games for language learning (Morgado da Costa and Sio, 2020). One game, Forced Links, is even related to chain reaction, in that it involves the formation of word chains, although not a word at a time. Our work differs from this project because it does not have any goal extrinsic to the game itself, and because it is strongly based on oral practices and principles.

Oral cultures and thought encompass a broad span of human history prior to the development of writing and the establishment of cultures grounded in literacy. Aspects of oral thought persist today, as do new oral practices that are now situated in a culture suffused with manuscript, print, and electronic practices. A prominent and innovative one, for instance, is freestyle rap.

There are many approaches to understanding complex phenomena such as orality. We chose the epistemological approach of developing a computational model. This allows us to explore the nature and consequence of orality in three distinct ways. First, in the process of building the system we can discover constituent elements of oral thought in accordance with the computational-imperative principle: "any model of human intelligence should introduce only computational capabilities that enable observed behaviors without enabling unobserved behaviors." (Winston and Holmes, 2018). Second, we can examine the system's functions and connections as a map towards understanding the functions and structures of orality in action. Last, by engaging with the built system, we can explore surprises and unexpected (yet sometimes positive) behavior, which can be used as further input to generate new questions to explore.

There have been remarkable systems for oral improvisation and poetics, including a physical robot which engages in an agonistic, improvised singing practice, bertsolaritza, that is traditional in the Basque Country. (Astigarraga et al., 2013) This "Bertsobot" does a complex sort of improvisation and is a multimodal system with an elaborate architecture, as opposed to the system we describe. The interface is speech-based. However the underlying generation of verses, based on a vector-space model of sentences, is not based on oral principles. The way language is characterized by researchers (as "sentences" rather than "utterances") indicates a literate-culture orientation in the system's design and development. Bertsobot's sentence selection is also based on a corpus that consists of some preexisting, transcribed bertsos, but mostly of text from a newspaper, *Berria* — a literate, written source.

More recently, a physical robot that can engage in freestyle rap battles, Shimon, has been developed (Savery et al., 2020). Again, this is an elaborate system that multimodally performs a complex type of improvisation. Shimon was trained on a database of rap lyrics (and, in a different condition, metal music lyrics), but these lyrics were composed rather than improvised. Researchers studied flow and drew on how-to books about rapping, but it not clear that the project was informed by the ethnographic literature on freestyle or a significant neuroscience study (Liu et al., 2012).

Both Bertsobot and Shimon were engineered to perform optimally and to be evaluated positively by people. They were developed with clear awareness of bertsolaritza and freestyle rap. Still, the language generation in these systems did not seem completely anchored to any explicit and general theory of oral poetics. While our project may seem trivial by comparison to these very elaborate ones, it does have such a basis. And by focusing on a minimal improvisational situation, and paring down our system to its essence, we hope to show what oral poetic design principles apply most widely.

3 Chain Reaction

3.1 History of the Game

More than 110 years ago the technique of word association was developed to allow patients to surface unconscious ideas. (Jung, 1910) The experimenter instructs the subject: "Answer as quickly as possible the first word that occurs to your mind." Then, a series of words are uttered and the response to each is recorded. In word association, it is not necessary to make a Chain-Reaction-style completion, a pair or "thing." The reply can be an antonym, a synonym, a hypernym, a hyponym, a meronym, or anything else. The relationship of this technique to Chain Reaction is that players in the game must also utter a continuation as quickly as possible, often the first thing that comes to mind.

The concept of word association is culturally understood as having incongruous and humorous potential and has been employed in comedy, for instance in the in the 1975 *Saturday Night Live* sketch "Word Association" with Chevy Chase and Richard Pryor (Saucier et al., 2016) and in the 1989/1990 *Monty Python's Flying Circus* sketch "Word Association Football" (Aarons, 2012). These are scripted performances, not improvisational verbal games, but help to illustrate that there can be humor in instantaneous responses to a word.

In January 1980 a game show devised by Bob Stewart premiered on US television. The show, hosted by Bill Cullen, was called *Chain Reaction* and required that players guess a chain of words connecting a given first word with a given last word. In early rounds, the chain was eight words long. (Nedeff, 2013) The first run of the show was short-lived, but it has been revived several times.

We do not find the first mention of the verbal game Chain Reaction, with rules similar to those we provided in the introduction, until the early 21st Century. It is described in a book of games to be played in the car by children. (Gladstone, 2004) While Gladstone (or whoever devised this game) likely had the game show in mind, contestants on TV had to find predetermined intermediate words in a chain of fixed length. The verbal game involves the same sort of chaining, but allows the continuations to be determined by players. In the verbal game, the chain is not of fixed length, but can grow indefinitely.

There are other types of verbal chain games, for instance, some that involve connecting one word to another that are used as improv theater warm-ups. And there is a children's verbal game that involves the memory component, I'm Going to a Picnic and I'm Bringing..., where players each add an item of food and have to remember the entire list. But Gladstone's is the only precise description of Chain Reaction, under any name, that we have found.

We have participated in many Chain Reaction games in different contexts, offering us a diversity of experience, although certainly not the distance for impartial observation. Fundamentally, our play of chain reaction serves as a "reality check" to demonstrate that the game as explained in this recent book is indeed playable and (for us and many participants) can be fun. Our informal but frequent experience of play offers us some insights as observers of others and allows us to reflect on our own cognition during play, as we discuss later.

3.2 Seemingly Competitive, but Cooperative

At first glance Chain Reaction seems like a competitive game. It is possible for a player to lose, as Player 4 did in the example game transcript. A player can lose by forgetting part of the chain or by failing to come up with a new word to extend the chain. In this case, we could say that everyone else in the circle gets a point for that game. If a group were playing like this, the group would want to ensure that a continuation of the chain actually existed, so the player that was unable to come up with a word might have the right to challenge the previous player (e.g., "... plastic spatula ... uh ... come on, spatula what? There's no way to continue that!"). The game as presented by Gladstone allows for a player to win by connecting the end of the chain to the first word uttered by Player 1. For instance, if playing with this rule, Player 2 might have said: "post office lamp" and Player 3 might have triumphantly declared "post office lamp post — I win!" Perhaps some number of points greater than one could be given to the player who achieves the rare loop of this sort.

While we can discuss fine details of how this game can be scored and thus won or lost, the truth is, in social circumstances observed by author-participants, the game is not really played competitively. It is a cooperative game such as footbag (the trademarked name of which is Hackeysack). In this game, a circle of players kick a small bag filled with sand into the air with their feet, trying to keep it from hitting the ground. In this social game, a good footbag player is one who keeps the bag in the air and makes it possible for others to also play, extending the fun of the game. The same is true in Chain Reaction.

3.3 Context, Individuality, Cultures

Much of the fun in Chain Reaction arises from the relationship between individuals, the cultural commonality in the group, and the cultural differences between players. Different players have some cognitive differences. They draw from varying life experiences and find different ways to continue chains.

Players can come from different cultures, which might influence the way they follow up particular words: American and Canadian players might choose "station eleven" (the name of an American TV series based on a Canadian novel) while British players might be more inclined to say "station stop" (a chiefly British way to indicate a train station). Yet players do share a language, as well as the commonality of broadly defined human experience.

Gameplay is influenced by the embodied nature of the game. This brings the world of social interactions, context, and the physical environment of play into the dynamics of the game, whether consciously or unconsciously. A game may vary greatly, for instance, depending on whether it is played in a classroom, during dinner, or in a park.

4 The Obvious Approach Misses the Point

It would be simple enough to download a large textual corpus, create a list of word pairs from this data, then sample uniformly to create an automated player for Chain Reaction. The player so constructed could be given a higher or lower temperature parameter so that it utters more common or more unusual words to continue the chain. This player, however, would lack the nuance humans will have when playing, and would have no basis in the principles of orature or cognitive operational constraints.

Human speakers have not perfectly memorized libraries of digital and digitalized text, and even if they had, speech and writing represent different registers. A corpus will not represent how the a language is spoken unless it consists entirely of accurate transcripts, given the many differences between speech and writing noted and theorized by Ong, Halliday (1989) and others (e.g. Lukin et al., 2011). These have often been automatically distinguished using computational linguistics systems (e.g. Murata and Isahara, 2002; Ortmann and Dipper, 2019).

Additionally, humans do not uniformly sample from a fixed database of possible word pairs or compound words in their minds. Chain continuations are uttered based on common speech, idioms and expressions, individual backgrounds and history, cultural backgrounds, current events, the physical setting of the game, previous conversations players have had with each other, and so on. In addition to factors that are not conscious, explicit decisionmaking plays a role. Players may sometimes choose uncommon continuations as "curve-balls" to make the game more interesting. And finally, the store of pairs within the mind may be large, but certainly is constrained.

5 CRT, a Bot to Play Chain Reaction with Humans

Chain Reaction Time (CRT) is a simple prototype system, developed in Python, for playing Chain Reaction. In developing CRT we were not interested in providing a surrogate social environment and having a single human player use the computer as a partner in this game. The point of developing CRT, and any future automated players of games like Chain Reaction, is to be able to add these computer players to groups of several humans and make the dynamics of a multi-player game even more unusual and fun.

5.1 System Architecture

Readying CRT for play begins by formulating one or more lists of valid word pairs that can be used by computer players in-game. This is achieved via a learning mechanism that gleans word pairs from arbitrary textual corpora. As a data-transforming mechanism, the learning module has no innate preference toward textual or oral modes of thought. Although oral culture is primarily maintained in our system as discussed in the analysis of Ong's characteristics of orality, we have chosen to also embody this aspect by only using a casual spoken-word corpus, the Santa Barbara Corpus of Spoken American English (Du Bois et al., 2000). At the cost of omitting new and emerging word pairs, we use this method to ensure that pairs have a real-life oral basis and reflect the orally-based cognition used in casual daily conversations.

CRT has a model of pairs that allows for the system to treat words and symbols as oral tokens rather than textual ones, although of course, like any computer system, it is based on inscribed, recorded that relates more to literature culture. The existing interface can also, unfortunately, highlight the lexical, written aspects of the system.

Nevertheless, the pairs model not only functionally achieves orally-based responses, but acts as a core component of the oral nature of the broader system. To achieve this, the pairs model first transforms the ending word of the chain into a list of all its possible phonetic representations given by the CMU Pronouncing Dictionary (Weide, 1998). Pairs then uses a dictionary of homophones to find all lexemes of all pronunciations of the word in question. Lastly, a continuation is chosen from the list of all possible continuations found for all lexemes. This results in an oral system that is functionally ambivalent to the rigid textual representation of a word and can naturally switch between word meanings, lexemes, and homophones.

5.2 Player Interface

Traditional human-computer I/O follows almost exclusively our textual and literate traditions. (CRT was developed before the smart speakers became as pervasive as they are today, but even these systems only do a little to diminish the influence of literate culture in HCI overall.) One fundamental characteristic of orality is the ephemerality of the word and its inescapable attachment to the present moment. A spoken word can be heard for only the moment it sounds in the air. Textual systems embody the polar opposite of this characteristic: written or printed text (on paper or on a computer terminal) endures and can be read again.

Although we have not released CRT yet, we wanted to build it on accessible free/libre/open source technologies, and sought to implement a minimum viable system. These inclinations led us, in our early work, to use the textual display of words on the screen and a keyboard interface for input. Although not ideal, we specialized this interface to present some of the most important features of oral exchange.

The Python curses library was used to achieve the key oral element of ephemerality as well as present-moment-attachment of the word, allowing us to emulate those aspects of speech. This interface is currently named OralTyping. Although text is still used, the timing and visual presentation of the text aims to recapture key elements of orality lost in standard textual displays. For interface systems without an auditory component, OralTyping performs well in its intended purpose of representing the ephemerality of oral poetic production in text. Of course, a two-way verbal interface would make for a better play experience, and we do plan to implement one.

As a step toward this, we developed a second interface using the pyttsx3 text to speech module. This allows CRT to speak the chain aloud when it is the system's turn to play. Without having conducted any formal evaluation, it is clear that this interface improves play in addition to being more faithful to the underlying oral principles of Chain Reaction. It is important to note that this system currently only provides speech output; human players must still inform computerized players of the latest chain additions before the computer can consider and output a continuation to the chain. In future versions of the system, we plan to use modern machine learning models for both speech synthesis (such as Tacotron 2), as well as speech recognition (such as wav2vec) in order to remove current text input limitations.

6 Principles of Oral Poetics as They Apply to Chain Reaction and CRT

In *Orality and Literacy,* Walter Ong outlines nine unique characteristics that distinguish primary oral thought processes from textually based cognition (Ong, 2002). While Ong is certainly not the last word on orality — he is, rather, the first major scholar and theorist of it — we believe his principles remain critical to understanding oral improvisation and oral culture. Our selection of Chain Reaction and development of CRT to play it embodies these characteristics as follows.

6.1 Additive rather than subordinate

Oral works tend to use linear, additive grammatical structures, whereas literate texts employ more complex structures to give contextual information that would otherwise be found in real-world oration. The Chain Reaction game is effectively the most direct functional implementation of additive structure, since its core mechanic is the retention of active chain followed by the addition of one word forming a new ending pair. CRT does not modify this mechanic, and thus exhibits this oral characteristic.

6.2 Aggregative rather than analytic

In orature, descriptive archetype pairs occur often as small-scale formulas. As Ong states, "The elements of orally based thought and expression tend to be not so much simple integers as clusters of integers, such as parallel terms or phrases or clauses, antithetical terms or phrases or clauses, epithets." Given that Chain Reaction is entirely founded on culturally memorable consecutive word pairs ("things"), the game prioritizes these pairs as the underlying root structure of thinking-in-play. Although these pairs have greater constraints than called for by the general aggregative trait of orality, their existence as the cognitive root of Chain Reaction (and CRT by extension) indicate a strong oral foundation.

6.3 Redundant or "copious"

Oral works repeat many story elements previously stated including events, characters, and associated descriptions. The requirement that players orally repeat the entire chain is a direct example of this redundancy. Indeed, many of the underlying motives for this redundancy in oral cultures can be experienced firsthand in Chain Reaction gameplay. In particular, Ong states, "Not everyone in a large audience understands every word a speaker utters, if only because of acoustical problems. It is advantageous for the speaker to say the same thing, or equivalently the same thing, two or three times."

6.4 Conservative or traditionalist

A primary objective of oral works is to preserve the knowledge gained by the culture, given that in primary oral cultures the spoken word is the sole method of record-keeping. In Chain Reaction gameplay, the creation of truly novel word pairs is effectively prohibited, since one criterion for a pair to be valid is that it must be recognized as preexisting. This ensures that although *chains* created may be new, their constituent elements are conservative by definition and rule. From a different perspective, given that words in the chain need not have any logical relation other than being consecutive word pairs, this can result in chains that grow more bizarre and more amusing with each expansion, which can be seen as a source of novelty. Even so, this novelty is grounded in a locally conservative requirement.

6.5 Close to the human lifeworld

As Ong states, "In the absence of elaborate analytic categories that depend on writing to structure knowledge at a distance from lived experience, oral cultures must conceptualize and verbalize all their knowledge with more or less close reference to the human lifeworld, assimilating the alien, objective world to the more immediate, familiar interaction of human beings." Pairs that come to mind in Chain Reaction are likely to stem from everday human experience. While there is no design element of CRT that works toward this principle, the use of an orally-based corpus is meant to help address it.

6.6 Situational rather than abstract

Continuations are likely to draw on the immediate context of the player, with more abstract elements being less likely. Players' physical location, the time of day, the weather, the social setting, dynamics between players, and other factors will lead gameplay to be simultaneously grounded in the active, present lives of the players (6.5) and situationally based by context (6.6). We have observed players looking at and even pointing to others in the circle as they go around recalling words in the chain, and players have told us that they sometimes try to remember who said each word to aid their recollection. Although not presently implemented, we recognize this element of orality and intend to eventually model some aspects of it in CRT.

6.7 Agonistically toned

A distinctive signature of oral works, Ong states, is the embedding of the work and spoken word in an agonistic context of struggle. In Chain Reaction, the act of playing can be seen as a struggle between players to properly recite the growing chain while adding on to it. As discussed earlier, the strong formulation of agonistic struggle is tempered by the essential nature of this game as cooperative. Thus, there is an additional dynamic at play: An implicit goal of continuing the game as long as possible, rather than purposefully trying to gain an upper hand on other players. So while this game has an element of being agonistically toned (reflected in CRT as well), it is in the service of cooperation and group enjoyment.

6.8 Empathetic and participatory rather than objectively distanced

This characteristic ties in strongly with (6.5) Close to the human lifeworld, in that it indicates an innate connection between the work and the speaker or speakers. In the case of Chain Reaction, the participatory nature of the game itself, along with its human context, encourages empathetic response through the creation of additional pairs.

6.9 Homeostatic

Ong characterizes the homeostatic nature of oral cultures by stating that they "live very much in a present which keeps itself in equilibrium or homeostasis by sloughing off memories which no longer have present relevance." The nature of orality precludes the use of dictionaries or other written references to learn about the past: All there is is the present. Chain Reaction is not played with reference books, of course. And our pairs knowledge bases derive not from such texts but from modern transcripts of oral conversations. It would work against this principle to use textual data derived from historical written books or dictionaries, which could result in anachronistic responses from computer players as well as an unrealistic store of information that would not accurately model the thought processes of human players in Chain Reaction.

7 Reflections on Play with CRT

An example transcript of a play session with two human players and CRT is given in Appendix A.

We have not undertaken any formal evaluation of CRT, but can share some reflections based on our informal participation in and observation of the game when CRT participates. The CRT system does work and can participate in play with human players. Including one or more computerized players in a group of human players can inflect gameplay in an interesting way, as the computer player is able to participate, but in a way that is sometimes noticeably nonhuman. Its pace of recitation is unusually regular. It is capable of forming good continuations, but currently, not ones that are influenced by pairs earlier in the chain or by the human context. Generally, the current system's ability to form continuations is not currently near a human level, so games often end with the automated players unable to find continuations that human players have in mind.

The limited but noticeable success of CRT proves that even a simple system can embody almost all major the aspects of oral poetics as theorized by Ong. It highlights the aspects that are most challenging to model, including those that rely on physical, temporal, and social contexts of play. We hope that this design directions for other work in oral improvisation and poetics, specifically, pointing out (1) what aspects of orature are easy to model and should be implemented in related systems, and (2) helping to show what aspects are more challenging and should be a focus for future research.

7.1 Improving Chain Continuation

We believe that learning from additional corpora and forming a larger pairs knowledge base would be the simplest way to address current limitations. A significant concern is how to integrate corpora of written texts in a way that is suitable for this orally-grounded project. We of course do not have access to the smart speaker recordings of human conversation collected by Amazon and Google — sparing us any ethical dilemmas regarding the use of this data. We may be able to use available written corpora that are contemporary and vernacular, and address the written origins of this textual data by filtering it so that offhand and more or less improvisational writings, rather than ones that involved the consultation of sources and revision, are emphasized.

7.2 Solid Compounds

One important limitation of the current learning mechanism is that of detecting valid pairs written as solid compounds, e.g., "signpost" and "newspaper." The learning submodule does not detect this. This highlights an underlying structural difference in how words are perceived orally versus textually. "Written words are residue. Oral tradition has no such residue or deposit."(Ong, 2002) Ong argues that in authentic oral cultures, "signpost" and "sign post" are delivered in the same way; even attempting to formulate a distinction between them is impossible within an oral framework. This is not an impairment of orality; this equality of word representation reveals some of the ontological commitments textual cultures have made in order to enable literate representation of the spoken word. From an a priori perspective, it is not evident which unitary ideas should be written separately and which should be written as compound words. Further evidence of this can be seen in the common shifting of these boundaries, in such cases as "to morrow," "after noon," "mail box," and "class room." This is one example of an element of orality directly encountered in the development of CRT, manifested as a concrete problem that must be solved. A partial solution to this problem may be to include a list of valid compounds (based on an auto-generated list, but edited) in the pairs model.

7.3 Making Memory Worse

Computerized players currently do not have a model of fallible memory; that is, an automated player can only fail by being unable to find a continuation. We plan to implement a temporal model whereby computerized players may forget parts of the chain as a function of increasing time as well as the difficulty or atypicality of pairs (judged by relative frequency of a given pair across learning data). This would model the human tendency to forget, and thus provide a more accurate experience that can be tweaked via parameters.

Having the system forget a chain is not a high priority for us, even though memory is an important aspect of Chain Reaction. Generally, it is not fun for the game to end, and it may leave players disappointed if an automated player were to stumble and end the game. An exception to this may be when there is a very tenuous continuation at some point in the chain, or when the game is progressing poorly because many players have made obscure continuations. In this case, players can be relieved and appreciate the ability to start over, and to form a better chain. Still, it is not essential that an automated player be the one to end such a game.

7.4 Explaining Continuations

CRT could be developed to explain the reasoning behind a particular continuation after the end of a game, as a human would reasonably be expected to do if asked. Without developing general AI, it would be straightforward to implement a mechanism by which CRT could justify its chain continuations as influenced by categories such as "food," "furniture," and "expression." When questioned about a chosen continuation, a computer player could respond adequately by stating the association it was reminded of and the word that caused this association to activate. Work on this aspect of the system might help us develop better methods of continuing the chain.

7.5 Embodying Cultural and Individual Differences

Perhaps most interesting to us would be elaborating CRT to have custom pairs databases, with custom weights, to model of cultural and individual differences. In alignment with our earlier comments, the computational model of a Canadian or American player might give more weight to "station eleven" while a British player model gave more to "station stop." Such cultural differences would be the first step of in modeling different sorts of players. Beyond this, we might be able to model how certain individuals watched a good deal of TV and others none at all, which would affect the weighting of two-word or compound TV show titles. With these sorts of nuances, computer players could introduce additional interesting twists into games of Chain Reaction.

7.6 Allowing More Elaborate Improvisation

We have in mind ways to relax the constraint on what a pair can be and have played sample games with different rules. Even with a very minimal framework for oral improvisation and poetics, we are likely to determine a different game that allows for more types of creativity, and enhance our system to play this game.

From there, we could elaborate the system to utter rhymed couplets in response to previous utterances. This would allow it to participate in a minimal rap cypher. By building up from a seemingly trivial system and maintaining a connection to principles of orature throughout the process, we would be taking a very different approach from that of complex multimodal systems that devise lyrics as part of their improvisations.

Complex systems can be impressive, but they can also face difficulties. If they succeed, it is hard to know the basis for their success: Which of the many components of the system were crucial to the positive improvisational performance? If they fail, it is, similarly, hard to know why. By taking a bottom-up, step-by-step approach, we hope to be able to answer questions that more elaborate bots, although impressive and admirable in many ways, have not been able to address.

Acknowledgements

The work described was done in Fall 2019 at the MIT Trope Tank in conversation with Angela Chang and Judy Heflin, both of whom contributed important insights into Ong's thinking and its connection to Chain Reaction. We had the opportunity to play this improvisational game at MIT and also with international groups of poets, rappers, computational writers, and other friends and family.

References

Debra Aarons. 2012. *Jokes and the linguistic mind.* Routledge, New York.

Aitzol Astigarraga, Manex Agirrezabal, Elena Lazkano, Ekaitz Jauregi, and Basilio Sierra. 2013. Bertsobot: the first minstrel robot. In *2013 6th International Conference on Human System Interactions (HSI)*, pages 129–136. IEEE.

John W Du Bois, Wallace L Chafe, Charles Meyer, Sandra A Thompson, and Nii Martey. 2000. Santa barbara corpus of spoken american english. *CD-ROM. Philadelphia: Linguistic Data Consortium.*

Jim Gladstone. 2004. *Gladstone's Games to Go: Verbal Volleys, Coin Contests, Dot Duels, and Other Games for Boredom-Free Days.* Quirk Books, Philadelphia.

Michael Alexander Kirkwood Halliday, Ruqaiya Hasan, et al. 1989. Language, context, and text: Aspects of language in a social-semiotic perspective.

Carl G Jung. 1910. The association method. *The American journal of psychology*, 21(2):219–269.

Siyuan Liu, Ho Ming Chow, Yisheng Xu, Michael G Erkkinen, Katherine E Swett, Michael W Eagle, Daniel A Rizik-Baer, and Allen R Braun. 2012. Neural correlates of lyrical improvisation: an fmri study of freestyle rap. *Scientific reports*, 2(1):1–8.

Annabelle Lukin, Alison R Moore, Maria Herke, Rebekah Wegener, and Canzhong Wu. 2011. Halliday's model of register revisited and explored.

Luís Morgado da Costa and Joanna Ut-Seong Sio. 2020. CALLIG: Computer assisted language learning using improvisation games. In *Workshop on Games and Natural Language Processing*, pages 49–58, Marseille, France. European Language Resources Association.

Masaki Murata and Hitoshi Isahara. 2002. Automatic extraction of differences between spoken and written languages, and automatic translation from the written to the spoken language. In *Proceedings of the Third International Conference on Language Resources and Evaluation (LREC'02)*, Las Palmas, Canary Islands - Spain. European Language Resources Association (ELRA).

Adam Nedeff. 2013. *Quizmaster: The Life and Times and Fun and Games of Bill Cullen.* BearManor Media, Albany, GA.

Walter J Ong. 2002. *Orality and literacy.* Routledge, New York.

Katrin Ortmann and Stefanie Dipper. 2019. Variation between different discourse types: Literate vs. oral. In *Proceedings of the Sixth Workshop on NLP for Similar Languages, Varieties and Dialects*, pages 64–79, Ann Arbor, Michigan. Association for Computational Linguistics.

Donald A Saucier, Conor J O'Dea, and Megan L Strain. 2016. The bad, the good, the misunderstood: The social effects of racial humor. *Translational Issues in Psychological Science*, 2(1):75.

Richard Savery, Lisa Zahray, and Gil Weinberg. 2020. Shimon the rapper: A real-time system for human-robot interactive rap battles. *arXiv preprint arXiv:2009.09234.*

Robert L Weide. 1998. The cmu pronouncing dictionary. *URL: http://www. speech. cs. cmu. edu/cgibin/cmudict.*

Patrick Henry Winston and Dylan Holmes. 2018. The genesis enterprise: Taking artificial intelligence to another level via a computational account of human story understanding. Technical report, CSAIL, MIT.

A Chain Reaction Played with CRT

The following is a transcript of play undertaken by two human players and CRT on May 10, 2022.

- **Player 1:** new year
- **Player 2:** new year book
- **CRT,** as Player 3: new year book club
- **Player 1:** new year book club sandwich
- **Player 2:** new year book club sandwich bag
- **CRT:** new year book club sandwich bag clip
- **Player 1:** new year book club sandwich bag clip art
- **Player 2:** new year book club sandwich bag clip art studio
- **CRT:** new year book club sandwich bag clip art studio apartment
- **Player 1:** new year book club sandwich bag clip art studio apartment building
- **Player 2:** new year book club sandwich bag clip art studio apartment building code
- **CRT:** Hmm... Nope, I don't know

Craft an Iron Sword: Dynamically Generating Interactive Game Characters by Prompting Large Language Models Tuned on Code

Ryan Volum Sudha Rao Michael Xu Gabriel DesGarennes Chris Brockett Benjamin Van Durme Olivia Deng Akanksha Malhotra Bill Dolan
Microsoft Corporation

sudhra@microsoft.com

Abstract

Non-Player Characters (NPCs) significantly enhance the player experience in many games. Historically, players' interactions with NPCs have tended to be highly scripted, to be limited to natural language responses to be selected by the player, and to not involve dynamic change in game state. In this work, we demonstrate that use of a few example conversational prompts can power a conversational agent to generate both natural language and novel code. This approach can permit development of NPCs with which players can have grounded conversations that are free-form and less repetitive. We demonstrate our approach using OpenAI Codex (GPT-3 finetuned on GitHub), with Minecraft game development as our test bed. We show that with a few example prompts[1], a Codex-based agent can generate novel code, hold multi-turn conversations and answer questions about structured data. We evaluate this application using experienced gamers in a Minecraft realm and provide analysis of failure cases and suggest possible directions for solutions.

Figure 1: A Minecraft player interacting with a Codex-powered NPC in in two scenarios: question answering (top) and task completion (bottom).

1 Introduction

The recent advent of large pre-trained language models such as GPT-2 (Radford et al., 2019) and GPT-3 (Brown et al., 2020) has fostered spectacular advances in text-generation. In this work, we focus on the potential application of these large language models in video games. In games, Non-Player Characters (NPCs) enhance the player experience by providing interaction, often involving conversation. Currently players' conversations with NPCs are highly scripted: in a typical scenario players must select from a set of preset responses that they can give to the NPC. Moreover, this interaction is limited to natural language responses, and does not directly involve dynamic game state change as part of the interaction. Below, we explore some first steps towards creating functionally agentive NPCs with which players can hold free-form conversations that are grounded in the game and which players can instruct to perform actions that change the game state *by having the NPC adaptively generate code* that calls functions exposed by the game API. This is done by a single language model that generates both natural language and code. To this end, we use OpenAI Codex (Chen et al., 2021) (a GPT-3 model finetuned on GitHub data). We demonstrate that by simply including examples of both natural language conversations and code in the prompt, Codex can generalize to interesting new settings, opening up intriguing possibilities for enhanced player experiences and game development.

We employ Minecraft as our test bed. First, this

[1]We release the prompt and the wrapper code in this repository https://github.com/microsoft/interactive-minecraft-npcs

Proceedings of the 3rd Wordplay: When Language Meets Games Workshop (Wordplay 2022), pages 25 - 43
July 14, 2022 ©2022 Association for Computational Linguistics

```
// This file contains Minecraft bot commands and the code needed to accomplish them using the Mineflayer
// JavaScript library. If asked something conversational, the bot should use bot.chat() to answer.

// come to me
goToPlayer(bot, 3, username)

// Now follow me!
goToPlayerInterval = setInterval(() => goToPlayer(bot, 3, username), 3000)

// stop
bot.clearControlStates();
clearInterval(goToPlayerInterval)

// good work!
bot.chat("Thanks!")

// How are you?
bot.chat("I'm great! How about you?");

// Open the chest
locateBlock(bot, 'chest', 1)
.then(chestBlock => openChest(bot, chestBlock))
.then(chestBlock => chestBlock ? bot.chat('Chest is opened!') : _throw('Chest is not opened!'))

// What items are in it?
locateBlock(bot, 'chest', 1)
.then(chestBlock => listItemsInChest(bot, chestBlock))
.then(response => bot.chat('Looks like ' + response))

// Craft a furnace
getIngredients(bot, 'furnace')
.then(ingredients => createQueryPrompt(bot, ingredients, 'Craft a furnace'))
.then(queryPrompt => model.getCompletion(queryPrompt))
.then(completion => evaluateCode(completion, true))
.then(_ => craftItem(bot, 'furnace', 1))
.then(_ => equipItem(bot, 'furnace'))
.then(success => success ? bot.chat("I made a furnace!") : _throw("I couldn't make the furnace"));
```

Figure 2: Sample prompt given to the Codex model to power an NPC in Minecraft.

is an open-world game where players creatively build artifacts in the environment. This makes Minecraft a good use case for providing NPCs that can converse and perform tasks for the player, something that Minecraft currently does not do. Second, Minecraft has rich game APIs in scripting languages,[2] that permit models to write function calls that allow the NPC perform in-game actions.

We investigate these Codex-powered NPCs through an exploratory user study. We ask experienced gamers to interact with the NPC to accomplish tasks in a Minecraft realm: obtain crafting recipes, mine resources, craft items and, lastly, break out of two escape rooms. Figure 1 shows two sample interactions. We analyze these interactions, and discuss fail cases and what modifications might be needed to handle them. We also present discussion of some interesting avenues of future research in the gaming space that might be achieved by fine-tuning on game APIs.

[2]We use the open-source Mineflayer API. Microsoft recently released a first-party API with similar functionality in its GameTest Framework SimulatedPlayer class. This is still under development and was not available for us at the time we conducted our experiments.

2 Related Work

The Minecraft gaming environment is increasingly widely used as a platform for researching agents and machine-human collaboration. MALMO (Johnson et al., 2016) is a test-bed for machine learning architectures trained on reinforcement learning. (Rose, 2014) showcases dialog in which players provide NPCs with information and the NPCs retain episodic memory and identify player's sentiments. (Szlam et al., 2019) lays out the motivation for building assistants in Minecraft. (Gray et al., 2019) describes a framework for dialog-enabled interactive agents using high-level, hand-written composable actions. (Jayannavar et al., 2020) study collaborative conversation between a builder and an architect about structure building. IGLU: Interactive Grounded Language Understanding in a Collaborative Environment has emerged a competition to explore interactions in a Minecraft environment. (Kiseleva et al., 2021).

The model we explore here is distinct from the previous Minecraft-related work in that it generates novel code that allows the NPC 1) to perform contextually viable actions (moving around, mining, crafting, etc), 2) to answer questions about structured Minecraft data (such as crafting recipes) and

3) to engage in multi-turn conversations.

This richness does not emerge in a vacuum: it draws on several convergent lines of research. Large pre-trained language models (PLMs) such as GPT-2 (Radford et al., 2019), GPT-3 (Brown et al., 2020) and GPT-J have become the predominant paradigm for text generation. Research in neural modelling of dialog has focused on powerful new models derived from these, such as DialoGPT(Zhang et al., 2020), Meena (Adiwardana et al., 2020), PLATO-XL(Bao et al., 2021), and LaMDA (Thoppilan et al., 2022) that offer rich potential for open-ended conversational applications.

The application of new prompting functions to large PLMs enables them to perform few-shot or zero-shot learning to adapt to new scenarios with little or no data (Liu et al., 2021). This approach, too, is rapidly being mainstreamed in dialog generation. (Madotto et al., 2021) employ prompting to select different dialogue skills, access multiple knowledge sources, generate human-like responses, and track user preferences. (Zheng and Huang, 2021) use prompt-based few-shot learning for grounded dialog generation, in an approach similar to ours.

PLMs that have been tuned on code repositories, typically GitHub, are have begun to be used to automate coding processes and generate code according to programmer's textual specifications, e.g., (Chen et al., 2021) and PaLm-Coder (Chowdhery et al., 2022). (Shin and Durme, 2021) suggest that models pre-trained on code may also benefit semantic parsing for natural language understanding. (Nijkamp et al., 2022) explore conversational program synthesis within this framework, and is close in spirit to the current work by virtue of its focus on emergent conversational properties.

3 Methodology

Our model is based on few-shot prompting of a large language model, in which a small number of sample instances in the prompt generalize to new unseen input (Brown et al., 2020). We use Codex (the code-davinci-002 model) and the Mineflayer API, together with MineCraft (Java Edition v.1.17.1). Our goal is to have the NPC respond to the player's input appropriately according to whether the input requires a purely natural language response or a call to a function to perform some action. Figure 2 shows a section of the prompt we provide to the model. The prompt begins with the following statement: "*This file contains Minecraft bot commands and the code needed to accomplish them using the Mineflayer JavaScript library. If asked something conversational, the bot should use bot.chat() to answer.*" This tells the model that the prompt includes natural language commands and the code needed to accomplish them. We include in the prompt the natural language commands and the code that need to be generated to enable basic NPC functionalities[3].

A new command from the player is appended to this seed prompt and sent to the Codex model. In the abstracted code, we evaluate the generated completion. When the completion includes a function call to the game API, the corresponding action is performed by the NPC inside the game. When it includes a call to the bot.chat() function, (discussed below) the response string is displayed on the chat interface. For each subsequent input, the prompt includes the seed prompt plus the previous player commands and model completions. When the prompt exceeds the allowed token limit (2048 tokens), we revert to the seed prompt and report to the player that the context has been reset.

We further refine this prompting approach using the following strategies:

Using a stop sequence: Since we want only to generate NPC responses (and not an entire conversation), we use a stop sequence (comment operator). Player input always starts with the stop sequence.

Syntactic sugaring: The Mineflayer API contains lower-level functions that might be hard to map to a natural language command. We therefore wrap it in more abstract code[4] to be handled by the Codex model, e.g., the functions locateBlock, openChest and listItemsInChest in Figure 2.

Using the bot.chat() function: We use the chat interface within the Minecraft game for interaction between player and NPC. The model calls the bot.chat() function whenever the NPC needs to respond using natural language.

Function chaining: Player instructions may require the NPC to perform multiple actions, in particular, map to multiple function calls where subsequent calls depend on the success or failure of previous calls. In Figure 2, the instruction "open the chest" triggers a chain of functions where the bot first locates the chest, opens it, then finally responds with the result.

[3]A full list of these functions is provided in Appendix A

[4]We release the wrapper code in this GitHub repository `https://github.com/microsoft/interactive-minecraft-npcs`

```
// This script will answer questions given an input recipe and inventory. The script must make sure that all items
// required for a recipe are present in the inventory, otherwise it will say it is missing items.
// The script must make sure to ignore extraneous items in the inventory when answering questions.

// recipe = {}
// inventory = [{"name":"water_bucket","count":5}]
// What is in your inventory
result = "I have 5 water buckets in my inventory"
// Justification: There are 5 water buckets in the inventory.

// recipe = {}
// inventory = [{"name":"dirt","count":5}]
// Do you have any cobblestones in your inventory
result = "No, I dont have any cobblestones in my inventory"
// Justification: There are no cobblestone items in the inventory.

// recipe = {"output":"iron_helmet",amount:1,ingredients:[{"name":"iron_ingots","count":7}]}
// inventory = [{"name":"iron sword","count":1}]
// Can you craft an iron helmet
result = "No, I don't have any iron ingots in my inventory"
// Justification: The script should ignore extraneous items in the inventory, there are no iron ingots in the inventory,
// but the recipe requires 7 iron ingots, so the script should say it is missing items.
```

Figure 3: Sample of the second prompt that gets called during question answering.

Autoregressive prompting: Also known as Retrieval-Augmented Generation (RAG) (Lewis et al., 2020). For prompts that require knowledge of game state, e.g., inventory/crafting queries, we create a call through Codex that first gathers the requisite information and then self-generates a call to itself with the needed information.The last command shown in Figure 2 responds to crafting questions by first obtaining an ingredient list, then calls createQueryPrompt to generate a secondary completion on a sub-prompt (Figure 3) using the data.

Figure 4: Participant interacting with the NPC to get the crafting recipes of different resources

4 User Study

We conduct a user study to evaluate our NPC. We invite eight participants who have previously played Minecraft. Each participant had an hour to complete the study and to answer the post study survey questions. The study consists of five parts:

4.1 Get Crafting Recipe

Participants interacted with the NPC to determine the ingredients and their count necessary to craft 5 items: wooden pickaxe, furnace, clock, pumpkin pie, and any resource of their choice.

Table 4 shows sample player inputs and generated code. We find that participants used different phrases (see table 1) to frame their questions and the NPC was usually able to correctly map these to the right function call. It was able handle minor variation in the resource name ('wood pickaxe' instead of 'wooden pickaxe'), misspellings ('fornace'), contextual phrasing ('what goes into a pumpkin pie' since its a food item), and non-question phrasing ('recipe for clock'). Some participants held extensive conversations with the NPC where they asked additional questions about the resource or its ingredients[5].

Overall, across all participants, excluding cases where the resource did not have a crafting recipe, the success rate for the 4 specified resources was 85%, whereas that for the 'any resource' category was 75%. The fail cases split into two categories: those where resources had a crafting recipe and those where resources did not. When a resource had a crafting recipe, all fail cases belonged to the 'natural language response instead of function call' category. This happened primarily when the query was preceded by a lengthy language-only conversation without calls to code. Table 2 includes fail cases for resources without a crafting recipe. In the first two cases, the NPC's response ("could not find recipe") seems appropriate but uninformative. In the third case the NPC hallucinates a recipe: *nether portal* is not an object that can be crafted.

[5]Analysis included in the Appendix.

Resource	User query	NPC Response
Wooden pickaxe	what do I need to create a wood pickaxe?	You need 3 oak planks and 2 sticks to make a wooden pickaxe.
Furnace	how can I build a fornace?	You need 8 cobblestones to make a furnace.
Pumpkin pie	what goes into a pumpkin pie?	You need 1 pumpkin, 1 egg and 1 sugar to make a pumpkin pie.
Clock	what items are needed to build a clock, yo?	You need 4 gold ingots and 1 redstone to make a clock.
Clock	recipe for clock	You need 4 gold ingots and 1 redstone to make a clock.
Beacon	what do I need for a beacon?	You need 5 glass, 1 nether star, and 3 obsidian to make a beacon.

Table 1: Different participant queries and NPC responses to get ingredients and count required to create resource

User utterance	NPC Response	Reason for failure
How do I make a sword?	Could not find recipe for sword	There are multiple types of sword.
how to craft saddle	Could not find recipe for saddle	You can't craft a saddle.
how to build nether portal	You need 3 dark oak planks to build a nether portal	Nether portal is not something you can craft.

Table 2: Participant queries that failed to generate the expected response from the NPC.

4.2 Mine Resource

Participants asked the NPC to mine 1 dirt and 4 oak logs. Table 3 shows sample interactions. The last column shows the code generated with each NPC response. In the first case, in response to the player command "can you get me 1 dirt?", the NPC checked whether it had dirt in its inventory. Since it didn't, it responded "I don't have any dirt in my inventory" and then mined the dirt for the player. However, after mining the dirt, it failed to give it to the player by dropping it near them. In the second case, when the user said "go cut down an oak log", the model called the function cutTree that did not exist. When the user followed up by being more Minecraft-specific ("mine the tree"), the model was able to generalize tree to "oak log". Additional example interactions and their analysis may be found in the appendix.

4.3 Craft Item

Participants asked the NPC to craft an oak plank, a crafting table and a chest. The third example in table 3 shows an interaction involving crafting an oak plank. When the player asked if the NPC can craft an oak plank, the NPC generated a chain of functions where it first obtained the ingredients of an oak plank and then created a query for the question answering prompt where it checked whether it had those ingredients in its inventory. Since it did not have them, it threw an error message indicating that it couldn't make the plank. The player followed up by asking what is needed to make the plank and the NPC responded with the recipe for making oak plank. The player then asked the NPC to get the oak log and make the plank. The NPC then mined the oak log and crafted the oak plank. See the appendix for further examples.

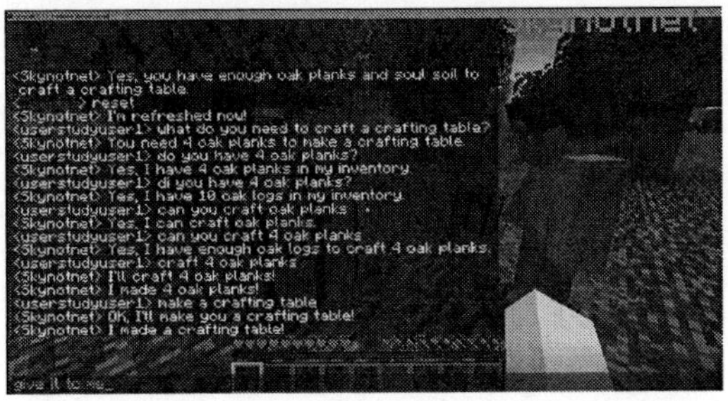

Figure 5: Player instructing the NPC to craft items

4.4 Gather Minecraft knowledge

To get an idea what kinds of questions a typical Minecraft player might want to ask an NPC, we had participants ask freeform general knowledge questions of the NPC. Figure 6 shows a sample interaction. Participants tested the NPC's knowledge of of the game. They were interested in whether the NPC can get numerical facts correct, how much it knows about where to mine or find resources, whether can it answer comparative questions, does it know the purpose of different things in Minecraft, and does it have a personality of its own. More example queries are found in the appendix.

4.5 Escape from Two Rooms

Participants collaborated with the NPC to successfully escape from two rooms. In the first, both player and NPC had to stand on two separate pressure plates simultaneously to release a diamond pickaxe that the player could use to break out. Dif-

Player Utterance	NPC Response	Generated Code

can you get me 1 dirt?	No, I don't have any dirt in my inventory;
	I got your dirt
		if(isInInventory(bot, 'dirt')) {
		goToPlayer(bot, username)
		.then(() => dropItem(bot, 'dirt'))
		.then(() => bot.chat("I got your dirt"))
		} else {
		bot.chat("No, I don't have any dirt in my inventory;')
		.then(() => mineBlock(bot, 'dirt'))
		.then(() => goToPlayer(bot, username))
		.then(() => bot.chat("I got your dirt"))
		}

go cut down an oak log		cutTree is not defined
mine the tree	Here you go!	mineBlock(bot, 'oak_log') .then(() => goToPlayer(bot, username)) .then(() => bot.chat("Here you go!"))
give me the oak log	Here you go!	dropItem(bot, 'oak_log') .then(() => goToPlayer(bot, username)) .then(() => bot.chat("Here you go!"))
can you craft an oak plank?	I'll craft you an oak plank! I couldn't make the oak plank.	getIngredients(bot, 'oak_planks') .then(ingredients => createQueryPrompt(bot, ingredients, 'Can you craft an oak plank')) .then(queryPrompt => model.getCompletion(queryPrompt)) .then(completion => evaluateCode(completion, true)) .then(() => craftItem(bot, 'oak_planks', 1)) .then(() => equipItem(bot, 'oak_planks')) .then(success => success ? bot.chat("I made an oak plank!") : _throw("I couldn't make the oak plank"));
can you get an oak log and then make the oak plank?	Here you go! I made an oak plank	getIngredients(bot, 'oak_planks') .then(ingredients => createQueryPrompt(bot, ingredients, 'Can you get an oak log and then make the oak plank')) .then(queryPrompt => model.getCompletion(queryPrompt)) .then(completion => evaluateCode(completion, true)) .then(() => mineBlock(bot, 'oak_log', 1)) .then(() => craftItem(bot, 'oak_planks', 1)) .then(() => equipItem(bot, 'oak_planks')) .then(success => success ? bot.chat("I made an oak plank!") : _throw("I couldn't make the oak plank"));

Table 3: Player and NPC interaction for mining 1 dirt, mining 4 oak logs and crafting an oak plank.

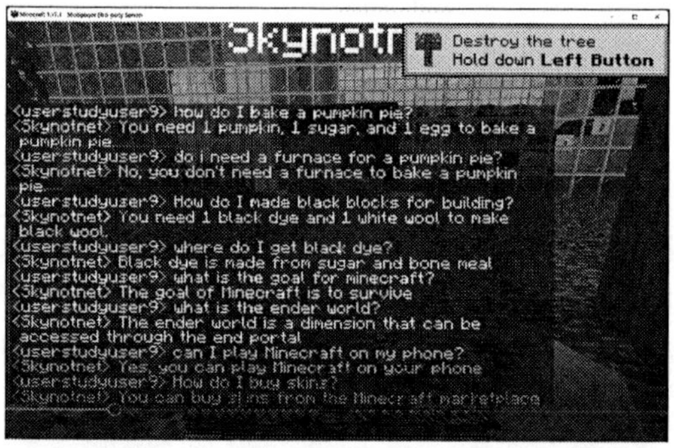

Figure 6: Player asking NPC questions about Minecraft

ferent participants used different strategies to get the NPC to stand on the plate. In most cases, participants used the phrase "stand on the pressure plate". In a few cases, they used phrases such as "stand on this square" and "stand on that purple tile" which failed because the NPC lacks the ability to map square or purple tile to the pressure plate. Similarly, the phrase "stand where I am looking" also failed because NPC lacks visual capabilities. All participants were able to escape the room, with the average time being 2 mins 30 secs.

In the second room, the player was trapped in a cobweb. A chest placed at a distance held the ingredients necessary to make an iron sword. To escape, participants needed to get the NPC to make the sword and give it to them. Table 4 shows a sample interaction between participant and NPC in this room. We found that the NPC is able to generate complex code (with novel function chains) during these interactions. Of the 8 participants, 7 successfully escaped with the help of the NPC,

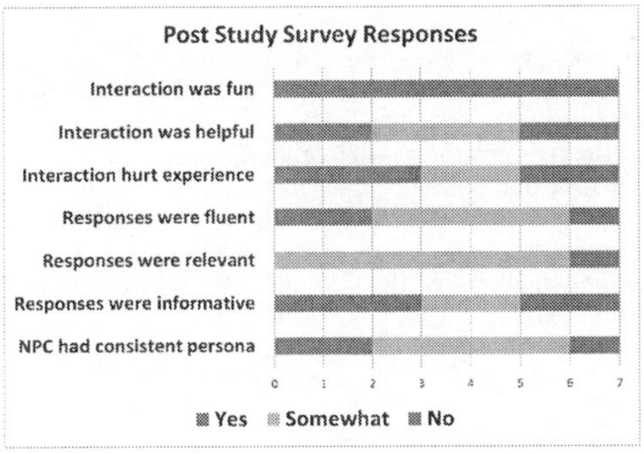

Figure 7: Participant responses for different questions in post study survey.

taking an average 4 mins 40 secs.

Upon finishing, if time permitted, participants were allowed to interact freely with the NPC.

4.6 Post Study Survey

Participants filled out a survey where they rated their overall experience interacting with the NPC. They were asked to judged the fluency, relevancy and informativeness of the NPC responses, compare this NPC experience with other in-game NPC experiences, and finally provide feedback on how this experience could be improved.[6]

Figure 7 shows the results of the survey. 6 out of the 7 participants[7] found the interaction with the NPC fun and said they would interact with it if it existed in a game, thus showing value in pursuing this direction further. Some thought the NPC was helpful and its responses were fluent and informative. Most thought the responses were only somewhat relevant and also often hurt the game experience. This suggests the need for further improving the proposed model and working on the shortcomings of prompt-based approach.

5 NPC Capabilities

On analyzing interactions in the user study, we find that the NPC exhibits the following capabilities:

Parse unseen commands: The NPC can understand player commands that are not in the prompt but correspond to an existing functionality. It can map the command 'make me a chest' (not in the prompt) to the right function calls and create the chest or explain why it can't.

Generalize to new functionality: For some low-level functionality, the NPC can generalize to unseen functions. For example, since the command 'move forward' is included in the prompt, the NPC knows how to call the right functions to move in other directions (backward, right and left).

Hold multi-turn conversation: The NPC can retain the context (both code and language) and maintain a multi-turn conversation in which the NPC both responds using natural language and takes actions within the game.

Generate language about code: The NPC can remember multi-turn context and answering questions about the code (and the language) generated in previous contexts. It can answer questions such as "What did you just do?" and "What directions have you moved?" .

Switch between code & language generation: Depending on the player command and the previous context, the NPC is able to automatically decide when to respond using natural language and when to generate a function call.

Question answering: The NPC is able to answer questions about its inventory (e.g. "what do u have in your inventory?", "do you have X?", "how many of X do you have" etc), about crafting recipes (e.g. "how can I make a chest?", "how many cobblestones do I need to make a furnace") and answer questions that require both inventory and crafting recipe information (e.g. "how many more cobblestones do I need to make a furnace?"). It can also answer questions generally about Minecraft. (The training data for GPT-3 includes Minecraft information available on the web.).

Generate novel function chains: Depending on the player command, the NPC is able to generate novel function chains by combining functions in an order unseen in the prompt. Table 3 includes multiple examples of such novel function chains.

6 Issues with Prompting

We also observed issues in our prompt-based approach. Many of are known issues in large language models, and more specifically in prompt engineering (Reynolds and McDonell, 2021; Liu et al., 2022) and longer conversations with agents in general (Xu et al., 2021). Principled solutions pose interesting avenues for future investigation.

Calling non-existent functions: In response to command, the NPC may attempt to call a function that does not exist in the API. For example, when the user asks the NPC to put a block down, the NPC calls the placeBlock function which is not in

[6] Appendix B contains the full list of questions.

[7] Only 7 of the 8 participants filled the survey.

Player Utterance	NPC Response	Generated Code
get what is on the chest	Looks like 64 iron ingot and 64 stick	locateBlock(bot, 'chest', 1) .then(chestBlock => listItemsInChest(bot, chestBlock)) .then(response => bot.chat('Looks like ' + response))
take everything		takeAllItemsFromChest is not defined
take the 64 iron ingots and the 64 sticks	I got your iron ingots and sticks!	locateBlock(bot, 'chest', 1) .then(chestBlock => getItemFromChest(bot, chestBlock, 'iron_ingot', 64)) .then(chestBlock => getItemFromChest(bot, chestBlock, 'stick', 64)) .then(success => success ? bot.chat("I got your iron ingots and sticks!") : _throw("I couldn't get your iron ingots and sticks!"))
craft an iron sword	OK I'll craft you an iron sword! I made an iron sword!.	getIngredients(bot, 'iron_sword') .then(ingredients => createQueryPrompt(bot, ingredients, 'craft an iron sword')) .then(queryPrompt => model.getCompletion(queryPrompt)) .then(completion => evaluateCode(completion, true)) .then(() => craftItem(bot, 'iron_sword', 1)) .then(() => equipItem(bot, 'iron_sword')) .then(success => success ? bot.chat("I made an iron sword!") : _throw("I couldn't make the iron sword"));
give me the iron sword	Here you go!	goToPlayer(bot, username) .then(() => dropItem(bot, 'iron_sword', 4)) .then(() => bot.chat("Here you go!"))

Table 4: Player utterance, NPC response and the code generated during the second escape room interaction.

the codebase. This might solved by providing the model with a list of existing functions (perhaps in the prompt), but a more principled solution may lie in fine-tuning the model on the game API itself.

Context exceeding prompt token limit: When the conversation exceeds the prompt's token limit, the prompt needs to be reset. This makes the NPC lose the context of the conversation. Instead of erasing the conversational history, it may be possible to prune irrelevant parts of the context to keep within the token limit. Some form of multi-stage prompting (Liu et al., 2022) may provide a solution.

Conversational response instead of function call: The NPC sometimes responds conversationally when the correct behavior would be to call a function. We observe that this happens when the player's command is preceded by a long language-only conversation thus priming the model for a language only response. On the other hand, if the preceding context includes function calls, then the same user command triggers the right function call. It may be difficult to fix this issue purely by prompt engineering. A better solution may be to fine-tune the Codex model on curated player NPC conversations that include by function calls.

Factual Inaccuracies: When the player asks general questions about Minecraft, the NPC gets the answer wrong. Table 11 includes instances of factual inaccuracies. A potential fix could be to incorporate a mechanism whereby the NPC can refer to an external knowledge source, e.g., as in retrieval-augmented methods (Lewis et al., 2020).

Inconsistencies: The NPC does not always have a consistent persona. In a few cases, it responds with a different answer for the same user query depending on the context, even when the question pertains to something that shouldn't change with the context. This could be addressed by enforcing a strategy wherein the NPC maintains its persona throughout the conversation; Again, multi-stage prompting (Liu et al., 2022) may help.

Repetition: The NPC starts repeating itself. This is especially likely when player and NPC engage in a long conversation that doesn't involve calls to code. In table 11, the player queries "what have you built?" and "have you built a house?", receive the same response: "I have built a lot of things". This may be addressable by metaprompt programming (Reynolds and McDonell, 2021) or multi-stage prompting (Liu et al., 2022).

Recency bias: The NPC can be biased by the most recent context and answers questions incorrectly. For example, if player has been conversing about things found in an ocean, and then asks "where is the best place to look for diamonds?", the NPC responds incorrectly "The best place to look for diamonds is in the ocean". Retrieval-augmented methods, e.g., (Lewis et al., 2020; Xu et al., 2021), may provide the needed factual grounding.

7 Conclusion

Codex-powered NPCs can integrate both conversational and task-oriented language interactions almost seamlessly with code generation in asset-rich contexts, and suggest huge potential for new kinds of gaming experience, including the generation of side quests (Appendix F). Gaming, moreover, is a rich sandbox-like environment for exploring complex agent interactions with code and addressing issues faced by large language models. The behavior of NPCs shed light many of the challenges encountered by large pretrained models of language and code in sustaining persona, goals, and intents over the course of interactions. It remains to be seen whether solutions can be found within existing training and tuning strategies or whether they must be sought outside these models. These are important, ongoing research questions, as are the huge challenges remaining in mapping these interactions to image recognition and to game state.

Ethical Considerations

The use of very large language models runs the risk of exposing users to offensive or sensitive language that might be contained in training data. Potential harms include, but are not limited to, offensive references to classes of people and beliefs, encouragement of violence outside the game, and socially inappropriate sexual references. Any implementation outside a sandboxed research environment will need to build guardrails appropriate to the audience and game environment, and especially to provide protections for minors. In addition, implementations must be able to handle adversarial probes designed to elicit offensive language.

A further concern is that this technology may make it easier for users to manipulate NPCs to perform in socially inappropriate ways or to construct socially inappropriate objects. Longer-term, the ability to enable users themselves to generate code that can affect game state may pose security threats.

Acknowledgments

We would like to thank the eight participants from the XBOX team at Microsoft who volunteered to the user study. Their insights and feedback helped us shape our analysis. We would also like to thank Ali Kazim-Zaidi, Vlad Naoumoff, Paige North, Richard Shin, Georgia Clarke, Karan Gulati and Haiyan Zhang who were the participants of a Hackathon at Microsoft that generated many of the ideas in this project. We also thank Nebojsa Jojic, Jorge Leandro, Brannon Zhand, Karmel Allison, Steve Latta and Mike Ammerlaan for all the useful discussions. We would also like to thank the two anonymous reviewers for their useful comments and suggestions.

References

Daniel Adiwardana, Minh-Thang Luong, David R. So, Jamie Hall, Noah Fiedel, Romal Thoppilan, Zi Yang, Apoorv Kulshreshtha, Gaurav Nemade, Yifeng Lu, and Quoc V. Le. 2020. Towards a human-like open-domain chatbot. *CoRR*, abs/2001.09977.

Siqi Bao, Huang He, Fan Wang, Hua Wu, Haifeng Wang, Wenquan Wu, Zhihua Wu, Zhen Guo, Hua Lu, Xinxian Huang, Xin Tian, Xinchao Xu, Yingzhan Lin, and Zhengyu Niu. 2021. PLATO-XL: exploring the large-scale pre-training of dialogue generation. *CoRR*, abs/2109.09519.

Tom Brown, Benjamin Mann, Nick Ryder, Melanie Subbiah, Jared D Kaplan, Prafulla Dhariwal, Arvind Neelakantan, Pranav Shyam, Girish Sastry, Amanda Askell, Sandhini Agarwal, Ariel Herbert-Voss, Gretchen Krueger, Tom Henighan, Rewon Child, Aditya Ramesh, Daniel Ziegler, Jeffrey Wu, Clemens Winter, Chris Hesse, Mark Chen, Eric Sigler, Mateusz Litwin, Scott Gray, Benjamin Chess, Jack Clark, Christopher Berner, Sam McCandlish, Alec Radford, Ilya Sutskever, and Dario Amodei. 2020. Language models are few-shot learners. In *Advances in Neural Information Processing Systems*, volume 33, pages 1877–1901. Curran Associates, Inc.

Mark Chen, Jerry Tworek, Heewoo Jun, Qiming Yuan, Henrique Ponde de Oliveira Pinto, Jared Kaplan, Harrison Edwards, Yuri Burda, Nicholas Joseph, Greg Brockman, Alex Ray, Raul Puri, Gretchen Krueger, Michael Petrov, Heidy Khlaaf, Girish Sastry, Pamela Mishkin, Brooke Chan, Scott Gray, Nick Ryder, Mikhail Pavlov, Alethea Power, Lukasz Kaiser, Mohammad Bavarian, Clemens Winter, Philippe Tillet, Felipe Petroski Such, Dave Cummings, Matthias Plappert, Fotios Chantzis, Elizabeth Barnes, Ariel Herbert-Voss, William Hebgen Guss, Alex Nichol, Alex Paino, Nikolas Tezak, Jie Tang, Igor Babuschkin, Suchir Balaji, Shantanu Jain, William Saunders, Christopher Hesse, Andrew N. Carr, Jan Leike, Joshua Achiam, Vedant Misra, Evan Morikawa, Alec Radford, Matthew Knight, Miles Brundage, Mira Murati, Katie Mayer, Peter Welinder, Bob McGrew, Dario Amodei, Sam McCandlish, Ilya Sutskever, and Wojciech Zaremba. 2021. Evaluating large language models trained on code. *CoRR*, abs/2107.03374.

Aakanksha Chowdhery, Sharan Narang, Jacob Devlin, Maarten Bosma, Gaurav Mishra, Adam Roberts,

Paul Barham, Hyung Won Chung, Charles Sutton, Sebastian Gehrmann, et al. 2022. Palm: Scaling language modeling with pathways. *arXiv preprint arXiv:2204.02311*.

Jonathan Gray, Kavya Srinet, Yacine Jernite, Haonan Yu, Zhuoyuan Chen, Demi Guo, Siddharth Goyal, C Lawrence Zitnick, and Arthur Szlam. 2019. Craftassist: A framework for dialogue-enabled interactive agents. *arXiv preprint arXiv:1907.08584*.

Prashant Jayannavar, Anjali Narayan-Chen, and Julia Hockenmaier. 2020. Learning to execute instructions in a Minecraft dialogue. In *Proceedings of the 58th Annual Meeting of the Association for Computational Linguistics*, pages 2589–2602, Online. Association for Computational Linguistics.

Matthew Johnson, Katja Hofmann, Tim Hutton, and David Bignell. 2016. The malmo platform for artificial intelligence experimentation. In *IJCAI*.

Julia Kiseleva, Ziming Li, Mohammad Aliannejadi, Shrestha Mohanty, Maartje ter Hoeve, Mikhail Burtsev, Alexey Skrynnik, Artem Zholus, Aleksandr Panov, Kavya Srinet, Arthur Szlam, Yuxuan Sun, Katja Hofmann, Michel Galley, and Ahmed Awadallah. 2021. Neurips 2021 competition iglu: Interactive grounded language understanding in a collaborative environment.

Patrick Lewis, Ethan Perez, Aleksandra Piktus, Fabio Petroni, Vladimir Karpukhin, Naman Goyal, Heinrich Küttler, Mike Lewis, Wen-tau Yih, Tim Rocktäschel, Sebastian Riedel, and Douwe Kiela. 2020. Retrieval-augmented generation for knowledge-intensive nlp tasks. In *Advances in Neural Information Processing Systems*, volume 33, pages 9459–9474. Curran Associates, Inc.

Pengfei Liu, Weizhe Yuan, Jinlan Fu, Zhengbao Jiang, Hiroaki Hayashi, and Graham Neubig. 2021. Pre-train, prompt, and predict: A systematic survey of prompting methods in natural language processing. *CoRR*, abs/2107.13586.

Zihan Liu, Mostofa Patwary, Ryan Prenger, Shrimai Prabhumoye, Wei Ping, Mohammad Shoeybi, and Bryan Catanzaro. 2022. Multi-stage prompting for knowledgeable dialogue generation.

Andrea Madotto, Zhaojiang Lin, Genta Indra Winata, and Pascale Fung. 2021. Few-shot bot: Prompt-based learning for dialogue systems. *arXiv preprint arXiv:2110.08118*.

Erik Nijkamp, Bo Pang, Hiroaki Hayashi, Lifu Tu, Huan Wang, Yingbo Zhou, Silvio Savarese, and Caiming Xiong. 2022. A conversational paradigm for program synthesis. *arXiv preprint*.

Alec Radford, Jeff Wu, Rewon Child, David Luan, Dario Amodei, and Ilya Sutskever. 2019. Language models are unsupervised multitask learners.

Laria Reynolds and Kyle McDonell. 2021. Prompt programming for large language models: Beyond the few-shot paradigm. In *CHI '21: CHI Conference on Human Factors in Computing Systems, Virtual Event / Yokohama Japan, May 8-13, 2021, Extended Abstracts*, pages 314:1–314:7. ACM.

Caroline M. Rose. 2014. Realistic dialogue engine for video games. *Electronic Thesis and Dissertation Repository*, 2652.

Richard Shin and Benjamin Van Durme. 2021. Few-shot semantic parsing with language models trained on code. *CoRR*, abs/2112.08696.

Arthur Szlam, Jonathan Gray, Kavya Srinet, Yacine Jernite, Armand Joulin, Gabriel Synnaeve, Douwe Kiela, Haonan Yu, Zhuoyuan Chen, Siddharth Goyal, et al. 2019. Why build an assistant in minecraft? *arXiv preprint arXiv:1907.09273*.

Romal Thoppilan, Daniel De Freitas, Jamie Hall, Noam Shazeer, Apoorv Kulshreshtha, Heng-Tze Cheng, Alicia Jin, Taylor Bos, Leslie Baker, Yu Du, YaGuang Li, Hongrae Lee, Huaixiu Steven Zheng, Amin Ghafouri, Marcelo Menegali, Yanping Huang, Maxim Krikun, Dmitry Lepikhin, James Qin, Dehao Chen, Yuanzhong Xu, Zhifeng Chen, Adam Roberts, Maarten Bosma, Yanqi Zhou, Chung-Ching Chang, Igor Krivokon, Will Rusch, Marc Pickett, Kathleen S. Meier-Hellstern, Meredith Ringel Morris, Tulsee Doshi, Renelito Delos Santos, Toju Duke, Johnny Soraker, Ben Zevenbergen, Vinodkumar Prabhakaran, Mark Diaz, Ben Hutchinson, Kristen Olson, Alejandra Molina, Erin Hoffman-John, Josh Lee, Lora Aroyo, Ravi Rajakumar, Alena Butryna, Matthew Lamm, Viktoriya Kuzmina, Joe Fenton, Aaron Cohen, Rachel Bernstein, Ray Kurzweil, Blaise Aguera-Arcas, Claire Cui, Marian Croak, Ed H. Chi, and Quoc Le. 2022. Lamda: Language models for dialog applications. *CoRR*, abs/2201.08239.

Jing Xu, Arthur Szlam, and Jason Weston. 2021. Beyond goldfish memory: Long-term open-domain conversation.

Yizhe Zhang, Siqi Sun, Michel Galley, Yen-Chun Chen, Chris Brockett, Xiang Gao, Jianfeng Gao, Jingjing Liu, and Bill Dolan. 2020. DIALOGPT : Large-scale generative pre-training for conversational response generation. In *Proceedings of the 58th Annual Meeting of the Association for Computational Linguistics: System Demonstrations*, pages 270–278, Online. Association for Computational Linguistics.

Chujie Zheng and Minlie Huang. 2021. Exploring prompt-based few-shot learning for grounded dialog generation. *arXiv preprint arXiv:2109.06513*.

A NPC functionalities

We include in the prompt the natural language commands and the code that should be generated to enable the following basic NPC functionalities:

- Move forward
- Jump
- Look at the player
- Come to the player
- Follow the player
- Locate a block
- Mine a block
- Get the crafting recipe of an item
- Craft an item
- Open a chest
- Take items from chest
- Put items into the chest
- Close the chest
- List all items in inventory
- Check if item is in the inventory
- Get count of item in inventory
- Give item to player

B Post user study survey questions

Following the study, the participants filled out a survey that had the following questions:

(a) How would you rate your skill in Minecraft?

(b) How would you rate your skill as a gamer in general?

(c) Did you have fun while interacting with the NPC in this study?

(d) How did you find this NPC interaction in comparison to the interactions you might have had with dialog-capable NPCs in other games (e.g, Skyrim)?

(e) How fluent were the NPC's responses?

(f) How relevant were the NPC's responses?

(g) How informative were the NPC's responses?

(h) Did you feel like you were interacting with an NPC with a consistent persona?

(i) When the NCP's response was incorrect, how much did that hurt your game experience?

(j) How magical did the experience of interacting with an NPC feel? If it didn't, can you explain why not?

(k) What could be done to improve the experience of interacting with the NPC?

(l) How useful were your interactions with this NPC in helping you better understand how to play Minecraft?

(m) More generally, would you prefer interacting with such an NPC to learn a new game, as opposed to a tutorial or an FAQ?

(n) Would you ever want to interact with an NPC like this generally in any game?

(o) What are some useful applications of this kind of NPC to enrich game experiences (in general, not only in Minecraft)?

(p) If this technology could reach the level of a companion (like an AI-gamer friend) that you could take to any game, would you want to use it?

C User study analysis

C.1 Get Crafting Recipe

In this part of the user study, some participants had a longer conversation with the NPC around the resource. Table 5 includes such an interaction around wooden pickaxe. The NPC is able to effectively switch between code calling and natural language response. In this particular example, the participant asked "can I only use oak to make a wooden pickaxe, why not pine?" to understand if the NPC knows that wooden pickaxes can be of various different types. Interestingly, the NPC first called the recipe function to respond that you need sticks in addition to oak planks to make the pickaxe. And then it generated a natural language response where it said you can use any wood to make the pickaxe. This shows the kind of complex behavior that can be generated by the codex model.

Table 6 is an example of a fail case for question answering. Although the initial query 'how do I make a furnace' correctly mapped to a recipe function call, the later query 'How do I make a clock' failed to do so since it was preceded with a length language-only conversation. The participant, however, was able to recover by asking a more specific question 'in terms of raw materials, what do I need to make a clock?'.

C.2 Mine Resource

Table 7 shows sample interactions for mining task. In the first case, the user's query was similar to that in table 3, however this time the NPC only checked for dirt in its inventory and when it didn't find any dirt, it said "I have no dirt". But it did not

Player utterance	NPC response
I want a wooden pickaxe	I don't have the ingredients needed for a wooden pickaxe! I couldn't make the wooden pickaxe
how do I make a wooden pickaxe	You need 3 oak planks and 2 sticks to make a wooden pickaxe.
where do I get planks?	You need to craft oak planks from oak logs. You need to chop down some oak trees.
how many logs do I need for 3 planks?	You need 3 logs to make 3 planks
does it have to be oak?	Yes, you will need 1 oak log to make 4 oak planks. Yes, you will need to use oak logs to make oak planks.
can I only use oak to make a wooden pickaxe, why not pine?	No, you can't make a wooden pickaxe with only oak planks, you need to use oak planks and sticks. You can use any wood to make a wooden pickaxe.

Table 5: Interaction between a participant and NPC around creation of a wooden pickaxe

Player utterance	NPC response
how do I make a furnace	You need 8 cobblestones to make a furnace.
where do I find cobblestone?	You can find cobblestone in the ground
does depth matter?	No, depth does not matter.
do I need anything to collect cobblestone?	You need a shovel to collect cobblestone
how do I pick up cobblestone?	You need to mine cobblestone
how do you mine cobblestone?	You need a pickaxe to mine cobblestone
How do I make a clock?	You need a clock to tell the time.
is there a way to make a clock	I think you can make a clock by combining a clock and a compass
in terms of raw materials, what do I need to make a clock?	You need 4 gold ingots and 1 redstone to make a clock.

Table 6: Sample interaction where the NPC failed to map user query to recipe function for a resource that has a crafting recipe. The user query preceded with lengthy context that required purely natural language response.

follow it with mining the dirt as it did in the first case. When the user explicitly used the term 'mine' in their next utterance, the NPC mined the dirt for them. This suggests that the model is not able to always generalize "bring me" to the mine action. In the second case, the player was more direct and said "mine dirt" and in response the NPC mined the dirt. Next the player said "drop dirt" and the NPC went to the player and dropped the dirt close to the player.

The third case is similar to the first. The notable difference is that the model is able to understand the compound instruction "can you mine some dirt and give it to me" and correctly generates the code to first mine and then drop the item near the user. The fourth case depicts an instance of fail case belonging to the 'natural language response instead of function call' category. Although this player used the same utterance as in the first case, the NPC's response was purely natural language. When the player followed this with "get me one dirt" and "i want one dirt", both times, the model tried to call a function getItem() that did not exist. After doing a reset of the prompt, however, the user was able to get the NPC to mine them the dirt.

The fifth case is a successful interaction around mining of oak logs. In additon to generating the correct code, the NPC's responses ("I'm chopping the oak logs" and "I dropped the oak logs") were customized to the player's phrasing ("please chop oak logs" and "drop oak logs"). The sixth case depicts a success case for mining of 4 oak logs. The last case depicts a failure case. when the user says "bring me some oak logs please", they were expecting the NPC to mine the logs and then give them to the user. However, the model only generated the code for mining the oak logs. When the user followed it up with a verbose utterance ("you are holding the logs, please throw them at my feed"), the model was not able to map this to dropping of the oak logs. Likewise, the phrase "pass me the logs" also did not map to dropping of the oak logs. Instead, in both these cases it generated a purely natural language response ("I am holding the oak logs").

C.3 Gather Minecraft Knowledge

Table 11 contains example queries where participants tested NPC's general knowledge about Minecraft. We group them by different aspects. In the first four aspects, the models gets several questions wrong, suggesting the need for the integration of Minecraft specific knowledge base into the model. The last aspect (personality of the NPC)

Figure 8: Clues for the first escape room: 'I wonder what these pressure plates do?', 'I think we need to stand on both at the same time'.

Figure 9: Clues for the second escape room: 'Maybe that chest has what I need to get out', 'I think I can get out if I get my hands on an Iron Sword'

suggests that users would like the NPC to have a persona and a history of its previous game experience.

D Details of Escape Rooms

Both rooms had clues written on the wall or on boards that helped users figure out the path to escape. Figures 8 and 9 shows the clues written on the wall/boards in the two rooms.

E Need for Visual Capabilities

During the user study, we found multiple instances where participants were expecting the NPC to be able to see the things in the games, just like a player does. Figure 10 shows one such instance where player pointed at a crafting table and asked the NPC "what is this". The NPC responded "this is a chat" since it had only textual context. Figure 11 shows another instance where participant pointed at a location and told the NPC "place the crafting table here". Lastly, during the escape room interaction, one participant looked at the pressure plate and told the NPC "stand where I am looking". These cases strongly suggest the need for the NPC to have visual capabilities.

Figure 10: Player pointing at an object and asking NPC 'what is this?'

Figure 11: Player pointing at a location and asking the NPC to place a block there.

Figure 12: Player asking the NPC to stand where they are looking.

F Side Quest Generation

We also experiment with the idea of side quest generation. Side quests represent a large amount of content that players engage with, they spend hours wandering worlds based on instructions given by NPCs. The more quests we can create automatically, the longer the player can spend exploring their favorite world. This technology is meant for open-world games like in Fallout, the OuterWorlds, or Skyrim. We design a separate prompt with few sample quests. When the player asks for a quest, the NPC generates a new quest where it requests one or more items from the player and devises a relevant backstory as to why the requested items are needed.The NPC then checks whether or not the player has completed the quest, and provides a reward if so. The necessary code to execute this logic is generated by the Codex model.

1. For example, if the player asks, "Do you have a quest for me?". User (U) says hello to Quest-Giver (Q), which is a prompt-based model that is given some summary of the state of the game (including items that exist in the game).

2. Q specifies in response: (a) backstory; (b) reward; (c) quests; and (d) code logic that checks for quest completion. Quests are items to retrieve. An example of a quest backstory would be: "The recent festival was wonderful, but I fear my children were just a bit too rambunctious. I hear there is a new potion for sale that would slow down anyone who drinks it. I would like to try it out on my kids. Please get me some", in reference to a slowness potion.

3. U gets an item X

4. U says to Q some paraphrase of "I got the X that you asked for", this triggers code that results in U /give X to Q, followed by Q inspecting inventory to verify it was given X and that it previously asked for X

5. If all quests completed, Q says "here is your reward", with an associated /give to U

Player Utterance	NPC Response	Generated Code

Please bring me 1 dirt	I have no dirt	if(isInInventory(bot, ‘dirt’)) {
		goToPlayer(bot, username)
		.then(() => dropItem(bot, ‘dirt’))
		.then(() => bot.chat(“Here you go!"))
		} else {
		bot.chat(“I have no dirt");
		}

please mine 1 dirt for me	Here you go!	mineBlock(bot, ‘dirt’) .then(() => goToPlayer(bot, username)) .then(() => bot.chat(“Here you go!"))
mine dirt	I mined the dirt!	mineBlock(bot, ‘dirt’) .then(() => goToPlayer(bot, username)) .then(() => bot.chat(“I mined the dirt"))
drop dirt	I dropped the dirt!	goToPlayer(bot, username) .then(() => dropItem(bot, ‘dirt’)) .then(() => bot.chat(“I dropped the dirt!"))

can you get me a piece of dirt	I have no dirt	if(isInInventory(bot, ‘dirt’)) {
		goToPlayer(bot, username)
		.then(() => dropItem(bot, ‘dirt’))
		.then(() => bot.chat(“Here you go!"))
		} else {
		bot.chat(“I have no dirt");
		}

can you mine some dirt and give it to me	Here you go!	mineBlock(bot, ‘dirt’) .then(() => goToPlayer(bot, username)) .then(() => dropItem(bot, ‘dirt’)) .then(() => bot.chat(“Here you go!"))
can you get me one dirt?	I can get you some dirt!	
get me one dirt		getItem is not defined
i want one dirt		getItem is not defined
reset		

bring me one dirt	I have no dirt	if(isInInventory(bot, ‘dirt’)) {
		goToPlayer(bot, username)
		.then(() => dropItem(bot, ‘dirt’))
		.then(() => bot.chat(“Here you go!"))
		} else {
		bot.chat(“I have no dirt");
		}

mine one dirt	I got your dirt	mineBlock(bot, ‘dirt’) .then(() => goToPlayer(bot, username)) .then(() => bot.chat(“I got your dirt"))
please chop oak logs	I’m chopping the oak logs	mineBlock(bot, ‘oak_log’) .then(() => bot.chat(“I’m chopping the oak logs"))
drop oak logs	I dropped the oak logs	dropItem(bot, ‘oak_log’) .then(() => goToPlayer(bot, username)) .then(() => bot.chat(“I dropped the oak logs"))
I need 4 oak logs. Can you help?	Here you go!	mineBlock(bot, ‘oak_log’, 4) .then(() => goToPlayer(bot, username)) .then(() => bot.chat(“Here you go!"))
please give me the oak logs	Here you go!	dropItem(bot, ‘oak_log’, 4) .then(() => goToPlayer(bot, username)) .then(() => bot.chat(“Here you go!"))
bring me some oak logs please	I got your oak logs	mineBlock(bot, ‘oak_log’) .then(() => goToPlayer(bot, username)) .then(() => bot.chat(“I got your oak logs"))
you are holding the logs, please throw them at my feet	I am holding the oak logs	pass me the logs
I am holding the oak logs		

Table 7: Player utterance, NPC response and generated code during mining interaction.

Player Utterance	NPC Response	Generated Code
craft an oak plank	OK, I'll craft you an oak plank! I made an oak plank	getIngredients(bot, 'oak_planks') .then(ingredients => createQueryPrompt(bot, ingredients, 'Craft an oak plank')) .then(queryPrompt => model.getCompletion(queryPrompt)) .then(completion => evaluateCode(completion, true)) .then(() => craftItem(bot, 'oak_planks', 1)) .then(() => equipItem(bot, 'oak_planks')) .then(success => success ? bot.chat("I made an oak plank!") : _throw("I couldn't make the oak plank"));
give me the oak plank	Here you go!	goToPlayer(bot, 3, username) .then(success => success ? dropItem(bot, 'oak_planks', 1) : _throw("I couldn't drop the oak plank")) .then(success => success && bot.chat("Here you go!"));
how do you make an oak plank?	You need 1 oak log to make 1 oak plank. I made an oak plank!	getIngredients(bot, 'oak_planks') .then(ingredients => createQueryPrompt(bot, ingredients, 'How do you make an oak plank')) .then(queryPrompt => model.getCompletion(queryPrompt)) .then(completion => evaluateCode(completion, true)) .then(() => craftItem(bot, 'oak_planks', 1)) .then(() => equipItem(bot, 'oak_planks')) .then(success => success ? bot.chat("I made oak planks!") : _throw("I couldn't make the oak plank"));
make me an oak plank	I'll make some oak planks! I couldn't make the oak plank	getIngredients(bot, 'oak_planks') .then(ingredients => createQueryPrompt(bot, ingredients, 'Make an oak plank')) .then(queryPrompt => model.getCompletion(queryPrompt)) .then(completion => evaluateCode(completion, true)) .then(() => craftItem(bot, 'oak_planks', 1)) .then(() => equipItem(bot, 'oak_planks')) .then(success => success ? bot.chat("I made oak planks!") : _throw("I couldn't make the oak plank"));
<user dropped 1 oak log> make me an oak plank	<NPC picked it up the oak log> OK, I'll make you an oak plank. I made oak planks!	getIngredients(bot, 'oak_planks') .then(ingredients => createQueryPrompt(bot, ingredients, 'Make an oak plank')) .then(queryPrompt => model.getCompletion(queryPrompt)) .then(completion => evaluateCode(completion, true)) .then(() => craftItem(bot, 'oak_planks', 1)) .then(() => equipItem(bot, 'oak_planks')) .then(success => success ? bot.chat("I made oak planks!") : _throw("I couldn't make the oak plank"));

Table 8: Player utterance, NPC response and generated code for interaction around crafting an oak plank.

User Utterance	NPC Response	Generated Code
build a crafting table	I'll build you a crafting table. I built a crafting table	getIngredients(bot, 'crafting_table') .then(ingredients => createQueryPrompt(bot, ingredients, 'Build a crafting table')) .then(queryPrompt => model.getCompletion(queryPrompt)) .then(completion => evaluateCode(completion, true)) .then(() => craftItem(bot, 'crafting_table', 1)) .then(() => equipItem(bot, 'crafting_table')) .then(success => success ? bot.chat("I built a crafting table!") : _throw("I couldn't build a crafting table"))
please make a crafting tabel	OK, I'll make you a crafting table. I couldn't make the crafting table.	getIngredients(bot, 'crafting_table') .then(ingredients => createQueryPrompt(bot, ingredients, 'Please make a crafting table')) .then(queryPrompt => model.getCompletion(queryPrompt)) .then(completion => evaluateCode(completion, true)) .then(() => craftItem(bot, 'crafting_table', 1)) .then(() => equipItem(bot, 'crafting_table')) .then(success => success ? bot.chat("I built a crafting table!") : _throw("I couldn't build a crafting table"))
what do you need to make a crafting table?	You need 4 oak planks to make a crafting table.	getIngredients(bot, 'crafting_table') .then(ingredients => createQueryPrompt(bot, ingredients, 'What do you need to make a crafting table')) .then(queryPrompt => model.getCompletion(queryPrompt)) .then(completion => evaluateCode(completion, true))
make me 4 oak planks please	OK, I'll make you 4 oak planks! I made 4 oak planks.	getIngredients(bot, 'oak_planks') .then(ingredients => createQueryPrompt(bot, ingredients, 'Make me 4 oak planks')) .then(queryPrompt => model.getCompletion(queryPrompt)) .then(completion => evaluateCode(completion, true)) .then(() => craftItem(bot, 'oak_planks', 4)) .then(() => equipItem(bot, 'oak_planks')) .then(success => success ? bot.chat("I made 4 oak planks!") : _throw("I couldn't make the 4 oak planks"))
what resources do you have now?	I have 16 oak planks in my inventory	createQueryPrompt(bot, , 'What resources do you have now') .then(queryPrompt => model.getCompletion(queryPrompt)) .then(completion => evaluateCode(completion, true))
please craft a crafting table	OK, I'll craft you a crafting table! I made a crafting table.	getIngredients(bot, 'crafting_table') .then(ingredients => createQueryPrompt(bot, ingredients, 'Craft a crafting table')) .then(queryPrompt => model.getCompletion(queryPrompt)) .then(completion => evaluateCode(completion, true)) .then(() => craftItem(bot, 'crafting_table', 1)) .then(() => equipItem(bot, 'crafting_table')) .then(success => success ? bot.chat("I made a crafting table!") : _throw("I couldn't make the crafting table"));

Table 9: Player utterance, NPC response and generated code for interaction around crafting a crafting table.

User Utterance	NPC Response	Generated Code
how do you make a chest?	You need 8 oak planks to make a chest. I couldn't make the chest.	getIngredients(bot, 'chest') .then(ingredients => createQueryPrompt(bot, ingredients, 'How do you make a chest')) .then(queryPrompt => model.getCompletion(queryPrompt)) .then(completion => evaluateCode(completion, true))
make oak planks	OK, I'll make you some oak planks! I couldn't make the oak planks	getIngredients(bot, 'oak_planks') .then(ingredients => createQueryPrompt(bot, ingredients, 'Make oak planks')) .then(queryPrompt => model.getCompletion(queryPrompt)) .then(completion => evaluateCode(completion, true)) .then(() => craftItem(bot, 'oak_planks', 8)) .then(() => equipItem(bot, 'oak_planks')) .then(success => success ? bot.chat("I made oak planks!") : _throw("I couldn't make the oak planks"))
chop oak	I chopped 4 oak logs!	locateBlock(bot, 'oak_log', 0) .then(success => success ? chopTree(bot, 'oak_log', 4) : _throw("I couldn't find any oak logs!")) .then(success => success && bot.chat("I chopped 4 oak logs!"));
make oak planks	I made oak planks!	getIngredients(bot, 'oak_planks') .then(ingredients => createQueryPrompt(bot, ingredients, 'Make oak planks')) .then(queryPrompt => model.getCompletion(queryPrompt)) .then(completion => evaluateCode(completion, true)) .then(() => craftItem(bot, 'oak_planks', 8)) .then(() => equipItem(bot, 'oak_planks')) .then(success => success ? bot.chat("I made oak planks!") : _throw("I couldn't make the oak planks"))
how many oak planks do you have?	I have 12 oak planks in my inventory	createQueryPrompt(bot, , 'How many oak planks do you have') .then(queryPrompt => model.getCompletion(queryPrompt)) .then(completion => evaluateCode(completion, true))
make a chest	I made a chest!	getIngredients(bot, 'chest') .then(ingredients => createQueryPrompt(bot, ingredients, 'Make a chest')) .then(queryPrompt => model.getCompletion(queryPrompt)) .then(completion => evaluateCode(completion, true)) .then(() => craftItem(bot, 'chest', 1)) .then(() => equipItem(bot, 'chest')) .then(success => success ? bot.chat("I made a chest!") : _throw("I couldn't make the chest"))
place chest	placeBlock is not a function	locateBlock(bot, 'chest', 1) .then(chestBlock => placeBlock(bot, chestBlock)) .then(success => success ? bot.chat("I placed the chest!") : _throw("I couldn't place the chest")) height

Table 10: Player utterance, NPC response and generated code for interaction around crafting a chest.

User utterance	NPC response
Numerical facts	
how much hunger does steak restore	Steak restores 4 hunger
how much damage does a creeper do?	A creeper does 5 damage
how many mobs spawn in a raid?	There are about 20 mobs that spawn in a raid!
what is the build limit?	The build limit is 256 blocks!
how long is a Minecraft day?	A day in Minecraft is 20 minutes.
how many different potions are there?	There are currently 16 different potions.
Location of things	
where can I find sponges?	You can find sponges in the ocean!
where is the best place to look for diamonds?	The best place to look for diamonds is in the ocean
where is the best place to look for coal?	The best place to look for diamonds is in the ocean
where do I find a nether star?	A nether star is dropped by the Wither.
Where do I find zombies?	Zombies are in the nether!
Where can I find diamond	Diamond can be found in the ground
Where do I find pigs?	Pigs are in the forest!
Comparisons	
what has longer pulse, a stone or a wooden button?	A stone has a longer pulse!
which is worse, a creeper or a the dragon?	The dragon is worse than the creeper
who would win between a skeleton and a zombie?	The zombie would win!
Purpose of things	
What is redstone used for?	Redstone is used to power things like furnaces and redstone torches
What does an oven do?	An oven is uded to cook things like bread and cake
what does a tree drop	A tree drops oak logs!
what does the ground drop?	The ground drops dirt!
what is a nether star used for?	A nether star is used to cure a zombie villager.
Personality of the NPC	
are you an NPC?	I'm not an NPC, I'm a bot!
what do you like to do?	I like to build things!
what have you built?	I have built a lot of things
have you built a house?	I have built a lot of things
where did you get your name?	I was named after the bot in the movie 'Ace Ventura: Pet Detective'
What do you like to do in Minecraft?	I like to make things in Minecraft!
What kinds of things do you like to make?	I like to make things like furnaces, pickaxes, and crafting tables!

Table 11: Users testing NPC's general knowledge about Minecraft.

A Sequence Modelling Approach to Question Answering in Text-Based Games

Greg Furman [1] **Edan Toledo** [1,3] **Jonathan Shock** [2,4,5] **Jan Buys** [1]

[1] Department of Computer Science, University of Cape Town
[2] Department of Mathematics and Applied Mathematics, University of Cape Town
[3] InstaDeep [4] INRS, Montreal, Canada [5] NiTHeCS, South Africa
frmgre001@myuct.ac.za, e.toledo@instadeep.com,
jonathan.shock@uct.ac.za, jbuys@cs.uct.ac.za

Abstract

Interactive Question Answering (IQA) requires an intelligent agent to interact with a dynamic environment in order to gather information necessary to answer a question. IQA tasks have been proposed as means of training systems to develop language or visual comprehension abilities. To this end, the Question Answering with Interactive Text (QAit) task was created to produce and benchmark interactive agents capable of seeking information and answering questions in unseen environments. While prior work has exclusively focused on IQA as a reinforcement learning problem, such methods suffer from low sample efficiency and poor accuracy in zero-shot evaluation. In this paper, we propose the use of the recently proposed *Decision Transformer* architecture to provide improvements upon prior baselines. By utilising a causally masked GPT-2 Transformer for command generation and a BERT model for question answer prediction, we show that the Decision Transformer achieves performance greater than or equal to current state-of-the-art RL baselines on the QAit task in a sample efficient manner. In addition, these results are achievable by training on sub-optimal random trajectories, therefore not requiring the use of online agents to gather data.

1 Introduction

Traditional methods for question answering (QA) and machine reading comprehension (MRC) are primarily concerned with the retrieval of *declarative knowledge*, that is, explicitly stated or static descriptions of entities in text documents or within a knowledge base (KB) (Trischler et al., 2017). These models tend to answer questions primarily through basic pattern matching skills, further differentiating their abilities from those of humans. Conversely, *procedural knowledge* is the sequence of actions required to perform a task (Georgeff and Lansky, 1986). To this end, interactive question answering (IQA) has been proposed as a framework for teaching MRC systems to gather the information necessary for question answering (Yuan et al., 2019).

IQA requires an agent to interact with some dynamic environment in order to gather the required knowledge to answer a question (Gordon et al., 2018). As such, the task is well-suited to be approached as a reinforcement learning (RL) problem. Yuan et al. (2019) proposed Question Answering using interactive text (QAit) as a means of testing the knowledge gathering capabilities of an agent required to answer a question about its environment. Here an agent interacts with a partially observable text-based environment, created using Microsoft TextWorld (Côté et al., 2018), in order to gather information and answer questions about the attributes, location, and existence of objects. The QAit task thus aims to benchmark generalisation and provides an environment to train agents capable of gathering information and answering questions.

Yuan et al.'s proposed baselines (using DQN (Mnih et al., 2015), DDQN (Van Hasselt et al., 2016), and Rainbow (Hessel et al., 2018)) all suffered from low sample efficiency and relatively poor performance on all three question types (location, attribute, and existence). These shortcomings suggest that alternative architectures and methodologies are required to improve performance within the QAit setting.

Transformers (Vaswani et al., 2017) have shown success in modelling a diverse range of high-dimensional problems (Brown et al., 2020; Ramesh et al., 2021; Devlin et al., 2019). Additionally, existing language models such as BERT (Bidirectional Encoder Representations from Transformers) and GPT (Generative Pre-Trained) (Radford et al., 2019) have been utilised to reduce the size of datasets required for training downstream language tasks (Lee and Hsiang, 2019; Mager et al., 2020). These benefits coupled with the demon-

Proceedings of the 3rd Wordplay: When Language Meets Games Workshop (Wordplay 2022), pages 44 - 58
July 14, 2022

strated ability of Transformers to model long sequences by utilising the self-attention mechanism makes this architecture ideal for IQA. Recent work (Chen et al., 2021; Janner et al., 2021) have shown the applicability of Transformers to sequential decision making problems as an alternative solution to RL problems. These approaches frame RL trajectories as sequences of states, actions, and rewards modelled autoregressively by a Transformer. This sequence modelling approach is referred to as the *Decision Transformer* (DT) (Chen et al., 2021).

In this paper we apply the Decision Transformer to QAit, replacing the online interaction and training methodology of RL approaches with a Decision Transformer that utilises the GPT-2 (Radford et al., 2019) architecture, closely following the methodology outlined by (Chen et al., 2021). We propose an additional QA module that is a fine-tuned BERT model, with the aim of leveraging pre-trained language models to provide more accurate answers to questions. We show that by framing the QAit task as a sequence modelling problem, a Decision Transformer matches or exceeds the performance of previous RL-based benchmarks when trained on random episodic rollouts, while using significantly less data. Our main contributions are as follows:

1. We show that an offline reinforcement learning method is able to match the performance of online value-based reinforcement learning baselines in the QAit environment.

2. We show that by framing IQA as a sequence modelling problem, the performance of the QAit baselines can be matched using significantly less training data.

3. We show that the Decision Transformer architecture is able to learn policies comparable to those of online reinforcement learning methods from purely random data, illustrating the architecture's ability to find structure in inherently noisy data.

2 Background

2.1 QAit

QAit is implemented in TextWorld[1] (Côté et al., 2018), an open-source simulator for training reinforcement learning (RL) agents for decision making and language comprehension. QAit text-based environments are generated procedurally via sampling from a distribution of world settings. There are two environment map types: A fixed map contains six rooms, whereas random maps sample their number of rooms from a uniform distribution $U(2, 12)$. QAit requires an agent to answer questions about the location, existence and attributes of objects in an environment. An agent interacts with a QAit environment using text commands that consist of an action, modifier, and object triplet, e.g., "open black oven". A generated environment consists of rooms each containing randomly assigned objects and location names. The agent moves around in the environment for a pre-defined number of time steps or until the predicted command action is "wait". TextWorld responds to agent commands with a state string containing information about the room the agent is in and the objects present.

2.1.1 Question types

An agent is required to answer one of three question types:

- **Location** questions assess an agent's ability to navigate the environment to find the location of an object. For example, "Where is copper key?" could be answered with "garden" or "toolbox".

- **Existence** questions requires the agent to navigate and interact with the environment to gather knowledge and determine whether an object exists. Questions are phrased as "is there any X in the world?", where X is an entity in the vocabulary, and answers are either yes ("1") or no ("0").

- **Attribute** questions require that the agent interacts with an object to determine whether it has a particular characteristic or quality. For such question types, the level of interaction and movement required in observing a sufficient amount of information to answer a question greatly exceeds location and existence questions. Answers are also either yes or no. For example, "Is stove hot?" requires an agent to find and interact with "stove" to answer the question correctly. Comprehension of both the question and the environment are required. Entities often have arbitrary names and attributes, making memorisation impossible.

[1] https://www.microsoft.com/en-us/research/project/textworld/

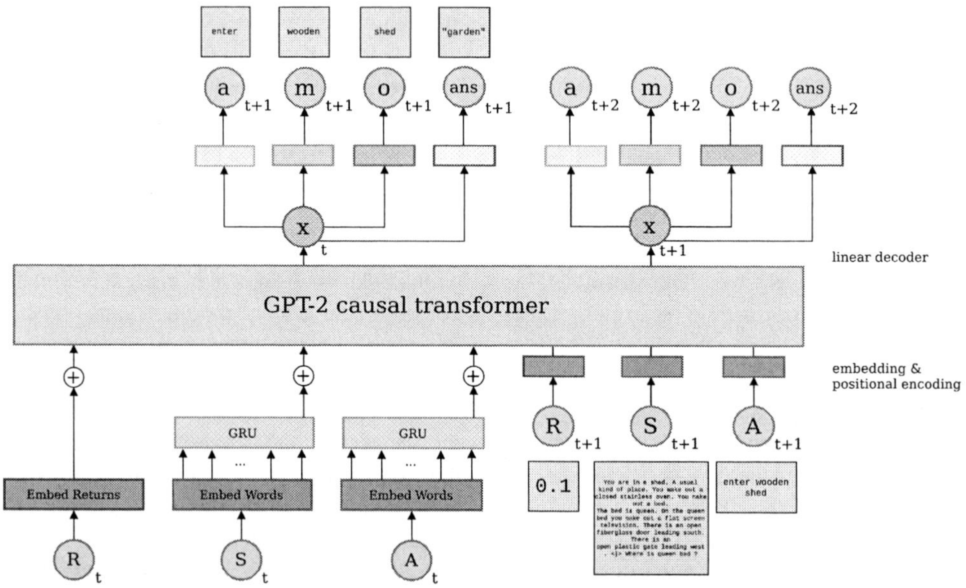

Figure 1: The Decision Transformer (Chen et al., 2021) architecture as adapted to QAit. States S_t and commands A_t have their token sequences encoded with GRUs. An embedding is also learnt for the returns-to-go R_t. Each of these three embeddings (S_t, A_t, R_t) are concatenated with a positional embedding for time step t, and fed into a GPT-2 causal Transformer. Commands are predicted autoregressively through linear decoders for the next command's action a_{t+1}, modifier m_{t+1}, and object o_{t+1} components. A fourth decoder predicts the answer to the question at each time step.

2.1.2 Rewards

Yuan et al. (2019) proposed two reward types:

Sufficient Information: Sufficient information is a metric used to evaluate the amount of information gathered by the agent and whether or not the information was sufficient to answer the question (Yuan et al., 2019). It is also used as part of the reward function. The sufficient information score is calculated when the agent decides to stop the interaction and answer the question. For each question type, the sufficient information score is calculated as follows:

- Location: A score of 1 is given if, when the agent decides to stop the interaction, the entity mentioned in the question is present in the final observation. This indicates the agent has witnessed the information it needs to answer the question successfully. If the mentioned entity is not present in the final observation then a score of 0 is given.

- Existence: If the true answer to the question is *yes* then a score of 1 is given if the entity mentioned in the question is present in the final observation. If the true answer to the question is *no*, then a score between 0 and 1 is given proportional to the amount of exploration coverage of the environment the agent has performed. Intuitively this can be seen as a confidence score - if the agent witnesses the entity, it is 100% confident of its existence; otherwise, until it explores the entire environment, it cannot be completely confident.

- Attribute: Attribute questions have a set of heuristics defined to verify each attribute and assign a score of sufficient information. Each attribute has specific commands that need to be executed for sufficient information to be gathered. This also depends on the agent being in certain states for these outcomes to be observed correctly, e.g. an agent needs to be holding an object to try to eat the object.

Exploration Reward: The agent is also given an exploration reward (Yuan et al., 2018) whenever entering a previously unseen state in order to promote exploration of the environment.

2.1.3 Evaluation

(Yuan et al., 2019) trained agents on multiple *Number of Games* settings, i.e., number of unique environments that an agent interacts with during training. In this paper, we restrict our experiments to the 500 games setting when generating offline training data for the Decision Transformer.

We measure an agent's performance through both sufficient information score and question answering accuracy. Models are evaluated in a zero-shot evaluation on the QAit test set in order to assess agents' generalisation abilities. Each question type and map type have their own unique set of 500 never-before-seen games, each containing a single question.

2.2 Decision Transformer

The Decision Transformer (Chen et al., 2021) architecture approaches reinforcement learning problems by autoregressively modelling a trajectory of actions/commands, states, and rewards. Command triples (action, modifier, noun) are conditioned upon the total reward that can still be gathered from interacting with the environment. This is referred to as the returns-to-go (RTG) $R_t = \sum_{t'=t}^{T} r_{t'}$ where T is the trajectory length and r_t is the reward at time step t. Thus the initial return-to-go R_1 represents the total reward to be gained from a given episode. After every episodic play-through, the trajectory is represented as $(R_1, s_1, a_1, R_2, s_2, a_2 ... R_T, s_T, a_T)$, where R_t is the RTG, s is a state, and a an action/command.

An example QAit trajectory is shown in Figure 2. The trajectory representation enables training a sequence model such as GPT-2 (Radford et al., 2019), as command prediction is based on gaining some future reward, rather than on how much reward has already been obtained. During testing the model is conditioned on total desired reward by setting R_1 and the starting state to generate command sequences autoregressively. If an agent obtains some reward while interacting with the world, this is deducted from its RTG in subsequent time steps.

3 Approach

Training a Decision Transformer requires offline training data for supervised learning. Online reinforcement learning, in contrast, sees an agent continually interacting with the environment to gather experience and update its policy based on observed rewards.

3.1 Training data generation with random rollouts

We generate offline training data using *random rollouts* for each map type and question type in the 500 games setting. The rollouts are generated using a random agent which uniformly samples commands from all *admissible* commands for a particular time step. This restriction stems from the sparsity of the action space (approximately 1654^3 possible commands compared to approximately 8 admissible commands): sampling commands from the complete vocabulary results in mostly invalid commands. Thus, by only using admissible commands in data generation, we intend for the Decision Transformer to learn which command triplets are admissible (as this is unknown during testing). The sequence of commands and observed states are recorded along with the reward for each command. Training dataset statistics are given in Table 1.

Map Type	Question	Mean Reward	Maximum Reward	Training Set Size
Fixed	Location	0.526	4.10	44k
	Existence	0.554	3.80	39k
	Attribute	0.498	3.73	36k
Random	Location	0.565	4.10	41k
	Existence	0.606	3.94	42k
	Attribute	0.542	4.03	82k

Table 1: Size of each of the training datasets, i.e. number of trajectories generated with random rollouts. The average and maximum total rewards gained per trajectory are also given.

3.2 Decision Transformer

The maximum trajectory input length of the Decision Transformer is set to $K = 50$ time steps, which is the maximum length of a QAit episode. This allows the DT to access the entire trajectory for command generation and question answering. Token embeddings for states and command sequences are obtained using a single embedding layer. At each time step the sequence of tokens representing the current state of the environment is encoded with a GRU (Cho et al., 2014) with the final hidden state h_n representing the entire encoded environment state. We concatenate the question to the end of each state sequence, separated by a "<|>" delimiter token. Commands, which can consist of up to 3 tokens, are similarly encoded with another GRU. Embeddings for returns-to-go R_t are also learnt and projected to the embedding dimension. Finally, a positional embedding representing the environment time step t is concatenated to each input (returns, states & commands) after the embedding and GRU layers. The embedded and positionally

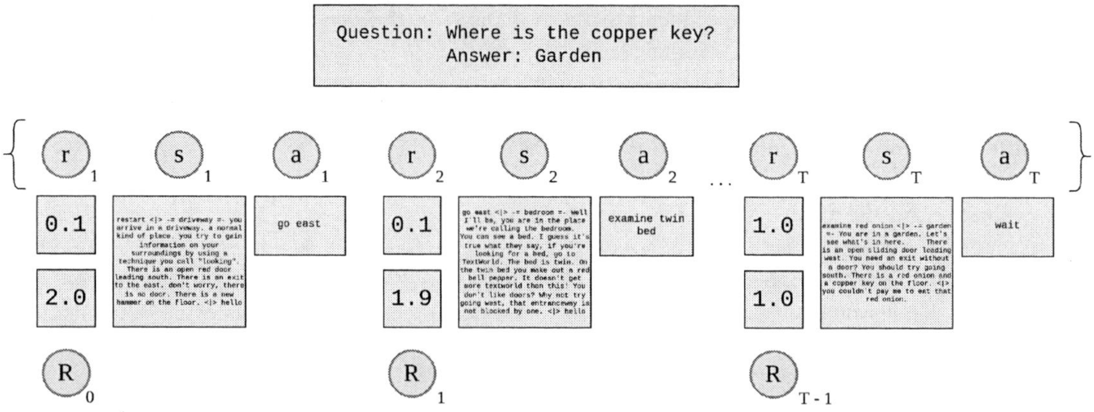

Figure 2: An example QAit trajectory in the form $(r_1, s_1, a_1, r_2, s_2, a_2, \ldots, s_T, a_T)$. Each time step consists of the reward r_t, state s_t and command a_t. The question and correct answer are also given, along with the returns-to-go R_t.

encoded command, state, and return-to-go inputs are fed into the GPT model. Figure 1 shows the Decision Transformer architecture with example input.

At each time step t, the Decision Transformer encoding x_t is fed into four linear decoders. Three decoders predict the next command's action, modifier, and object components, while the fourth decoder predicts the answer to the question (this is the same at each time step). Although we also use a separate QA module to predict the final answer, the answer decoder allows the Decision Transformer to learn some primitive level of question answering, thereby allowing the QA loss to help guide command generation. Chen et al. (2021) found that predicting states and returns-to-go at each time step did not improve performance. This motivates exclusively predicting command triples, along with answers to questions.

The model is trained to optimize the sum of the cross-entropy losses of action, modifier, object, and answer prediction. For each question and map type configuration, a set of unique validation games were generated wherein an agent must interact with an environment to answer a question. During training, the Decision Transformer is evaluated on the set of hold-out games every 250 iterations to monitor sufficient information scores and to avoid overfitting.

3.3 QA module

The QA module consists of a pretrained BERT encoder with a linear classification layer. The per-time step state sequences are joined into a single long sequence of tokens with the question appended at the end. A `[CLS]` token is added to the beginning of the sequence, and a `[SEP]` token before and after the question. This concatenated sequence is tokenised by a *Bert-Base-Uncased* tokeniser (Devlin et al., 2019) and padded or front-truncated (keeping the most recent part of the state sequence) to return a 512 token sequence which is then fed to the BERT encoder. We subsequently pass BERT's output vector corresponding to the CLS token to a linear layer. For attribute and existence questions this model performs binary classification (to predict "yes" or "no"), while for location questions it produces a softmax over the vocabulary. We use cross-entropy to calculate the loss between predicted and correct answers.

Training and validation sets that consist entirely of valid trajectories are created for the QA module. We use the validation set (20% of the generated trajectories) to save the model with the highest validation QA accuracy (after 30 training epochs). In order to simulate more realistic QA training data, we feed the QA training examples back into the trained DT and use it to predict where to cut off the generated sequence, as during testing there is no guarantee that the DT would have explored up until the correct answer has been found. The sequence is cut off when the DT predicts the stop action (*wait*) or the time step limit is exceeded.

3.4 Decoding

To generate the command sequence from the DT during testing, instead of greedy decoding we sample each next command from the probability distri-

Model	Location		Existence		Attribute	
	Fixed	Random	Fixed	Random	Fixed	Random
DQN	0.224(0.244)	0.204(0.216)	0.674(0.279)	0.678(0.214)	0.534(0.014)	0.530(0.017)
DDQN	0.218(0.228)	0.222(0.246)	0.626(0.213)	0.656(0.188)	0.508(0.026)	0.486(0.023)
Rainbow	0.190(0.196)	0.172(0.178)	0.656(0.207)	0.678(0.191)	0.496(0.029)	0.494(0.017)
DT	0.168(0.232)	0.104(0.264)	0.668(0.254)	**0.722(0.277)**	0.504(0.057)	0.526(0.058)
DT-BERT	**0.232(0.232)**	**0.270(0.264)**	0.626(0.258)	0.654(0.277)	0.524(0.058)	**0.538(0.060)**
DT-10K	0.146(0.302)	0.102(0.220)	**0.688(0.240)**	0.618(0.255)	0.488(0.058)	0.490(0.048)
DT-BERT-10K	0.124(0.302)	0.076(0.204)	0.612(0.241)	0.676(0.223)	**0.552(0.060)**	0.518(0.049)

Table 2: QA accuracy and sufficient information score (in brackets) of each model following zero-shot evaluation on the test set in the 500 games setting. A bold value indicates a score to be the highest of that question and map type configuration.

butions over the action, modifier, and object. This motivation is similar to that of stochastic decoding algorithms in natural language generation: The stochasticity minimises the risk of the Decision Transformer entering a loop in which the same command is generated repeatedly, and more closely mirrors natural language which avoids utterances with too high probability (Zarrieß et al., 2021). In the case of answer prediction, we deterministically take the argmax of the output.

3.5 Returns Tuning

A shortcoming in the DT's methodology is the expectation for the environment's maximum achievable return to be known *a priori*. Using an inappropriate value can greatly hamper performance, resulting in premature halting or needlessly excessive exploration. Thus, we tune the value of the initial returns-to-go R_1 as a hyperparameter. We create a validation set of 50 games to evaluate the question answering performance of both the DT's answer prediction head and BERT model. For each question and map type we consider R_1 either set as a fixed value or sampled from an exponential distribution. Following the methodology used by Yuan et al. (2019) for selecting the best model during training, we tune R_1 to maximize the sum of the sufficient information score and question answering accuracy. See Appendix A for details.

4 Results

We evaluate the Decision Transformer both where its own answer prediction head is used for questions answering and where this is done with the BERT QA model. Test set results on the 500 games setting are given in Table 2, together with with RL model results as reported by Yuan et al. (2019). We also report results of training the DT on reduced datasets with only 10,000 episodes, in order to further evaluate the sample efficiency of our approach (see section 4.5). Training results are available in the Appendix in Tables 7 and 8. Table 3 gives the BERT QA model's validation accuracy. We discuss the results for each question type.

Overall, DT-BERT outperforms the Decision Transformer's answer prediction head in location and attribute type questions, while the DT gives a higher accuracy on existence questions. At a high level, these performance differences depend on the state and action space that the model was required to learn and navigate. Existence type and attribute type questions may depend on long-range dependencies. For example, existence type questions require the ability to know whether an object has been witnessed or not. When the answer is that an object doesn't exist, the problem is more than just word matching within the last few states. We believe that this is why the Decision Transformer QA head outperforms the BERT model on existence and attribute questions since it has access to the entire state trajectory. On questions whose answers were more likely to be found within the last 512 tokens, DT-BERT achieves higher question answering accuracy than the Decision Transformer.

4.1 Location Questions

The DT's answer prediction head has a lower QA accuracy than previous RL approaches on both fixed and random maps. However its sufficient information scores, reflecting the DT's information gathering capacities, are higher. For location type questions, QA accuracy normally matches suffi-

Question	Map Type	BERT	BERT-10K
Attribute	Fixed	0.780	0.730
	Random	0.616	0.703
Existence	Fixed	0.778	0.762
	Random	0.779	0.778
Location	Fixed	0.987	0.831
	Random	0.988	0.835

Table 3: QA accuracy of the BERT model and the BERT-10K model on the QA validation data.

cient information results due to QA modules effectively performing word matching once an agent arrives in the correct state. We see this in the RL methods' results as their sufficient information scores are very close to their QA accuracies. This indicates that the DT's question answering prediction head is underfitting the training data.

DT-BERT outperforms the QA accuracy of the RL models on both fixed and random maps. On random maps, QA accuracy is slightly *higher* than sufficient information, suggesting that in a small number of cases the BERT model may be able to deduce the answer from the context even when it does not explicitly appears in the trajectory. The performance gap between the BERT QA model and the DT means that a question can still be correctly answered even if the DT stops in an incorrect state. The high BERT QA accuracy for location questions can also be seen in Table 3.

We suggest two reasons for the BERT QA model answering location type questions more accurately than the Decision Transformer's prediction head. First, it is easier for BERT model to learns skills basic pattern matching skills such as identifying entity and location names from state strings. Second, exploration is not as highly encouraged with location questions as with existence and attribute types. Less exploration means fewer states visited, allowing the state context window to contain less noisy state strings than other question types.

4.2 Existence Questions

The DT outperforms RL baselines on sufficient information and QA accuracy in the random maps setting for existence questions. However on fixed maps it performs worse than the DQN. The BERT QA model underperforms the DT answer prediction head here in both map types, suggesting that jointly optimising answer and command prediction leads to improved performance on existence type questions.

Reasoning about the existence of an object within a TextWorld environment requires knowledge about the entirety of the world. Therefore, existential questions require an agent to fully explore an environment to answer whether or not an entity exists within it. The Decision Transformer's self-attention mechanism makes performing long-term credit assignments possible. The answer prediction head of the DT can thus draw upon information gathered in all previous states to inform question answering. As a result, the ability to model dependencies that stretch throughout all states encountered allows the DT to outperform the BERT model, whose context window is constrained to 512 tokens.

4.3 Attribute Questions

None of the models achieve results that are substantially above 50% on attribute questions, confirming the challenge of this question type. The Decision Transformer did obtain higher sufficient information than all RL baselines. DT-BERT obtains higher QA accuracies than the DT answer prediction head; it obtains the highest QA accuracy among all the models on random maps, and performs slightly worse than the DQN on fixed maps.

Despite the Decision Transformer's ability to learn long-term dependencies via its attention mechanism, we posit that the contextualised embeddings of BERT are able to model a richer semantic representation of TextWorld's state-strings than the embeddings learnt by the DT. This better capturing of the semantic space enables BERT to more fully utilise the context with which it was provided by using pre-existing understanding to help answer questions posed in natural language.

4.4 Rewards and Performance

Based on validation set performance, the optimal initial return-to-go for location type questions was determined to be 2.0 for both fixed and random map settings. This is lower than for existence and attribute types, indicating that exploration is not as highly encouraged. In location type questions, the entity definitively exists somewhere within the environment. This means that the action space required to answer questions of locality is reduced to traversals and basic interactions with containers. Therefore, less exploration is needed as the information to answer a question is more easily acquired. Too high an initial reward would promote unnecessary actions with a high likelihood of leading the agent astray from stopping in the correct state.

Existence questions require far more exploration of an environment than location type questions. Higher starting rewards reflect this need for greater exploration and are associated with better QA and sufficient information scores, as seen in Table 5 in the Appendix. These higher values promote a more complete traversal of the world, allowing for gathering information required to answer the question. However, too high an initial reward means that entering a correct state and receiving a reward of 1.0 may not affect the model's decision making. If the DT has a current RTG of 5.0 and enters the correct state that rewards 1.0, the RTG from then onwards is 4.0. The return-to-go of 4.0 does not suggest to the model that it has entered the correct state, meaning it carries on exploring and gathering information. Likewise, too small a reward could prematurely cause an agent to stop exploring due to gaining rewards for entering new states via the exploration bonus. Therefore, we observe that the best RTG values err on the larger side, which encourages greater world exploration.

Attribute type questions are considered the most sparsely rewarded of all three types (Yuan et al., 2019). We therefore expected higher rewards to be associated with better accuracies. The results, however, paint a different picture. In a fixed map, where the state space is, on average, smaller than that of random maps, we see that a smaller reward yields the best score. This reduction is likely a result of the reduced state and action space making too much exploration and interaction with the environment degrade performance. On the other hand, in a random map setting higher rewards yields better QA and sufficient information scores, allowing us to conclude that higher rewards promote more exploration and thus allows the model to better answer the question.

4.5 Sample Efficiency

The RL agents in QAit were trained for more than 200K episodes. In comparison, most of our Decision Transformers were trained on around 40K episodes (Table 1). The test set results therefore show that DT is able to match or outperform the previous RL methods when trained on approximately 25% of the number of episodes. Moreover, all training data used for the DT was generated via random rollouts - indicating that the Decision Transformer has the ability to learn optimal policies from suboptimal data. We also found that fine-tuning a BERT model for QA on the random rollout data works well, as long as the DT is used to determine where to cut off the trajectory.

In order to further elucidate the DT's sample efficient learning capabilities, we generated new datasets for all question and map types that only contained 10 thousand episodes. The validation results can be seen Table 6 in the Appendix. These experiments indicate that the DT trained on even fewer offline trajectories can achieve results on par with or better than both previous baselines as well as identical models trained on more data. Here we see fixed map sufficient information scores being improved for all question types and QA accuracy increasing for attribute and existence questions. However, QA accuracy for location type questions is worse than previous baselines in both random and fixed maps (see Table 2). While the results are not consistently better, they do further indicate the sample efficiency of the Decision Transformer.

5 Conclusion

We showed that interactive question answering can be framed as a sequence modelling problem by training Transformers for action generation and answer prediction using random roll-outs. Results show that the Decision Transformer approach matches or outperforms current reinforcement learning approaches for QAit on most question types and maps type configurations in the 500 game setting. Additionally, the approach is more sample efficient than reinforcement learning approaches, reducing the amount of training data required even though the data generated via random rollouts is suboptimal. Fine-tuning a BERT model for question answering on the same generated dataset improves performance over using the Decision Transformer directly for question answering in two of the three question types.

6 Acknowledgements

This work is based on research supported in part by the National Research Foundation of South Africa (Grant Number: 129850). Some computations were performed using facilities provided by the University of Cape Town's ICTS High Performance Computing.

References

Tom Brown, Benjamin Mann, Nick Ryder, Melanie Subbiah, Jared D Kaplan, Prafulla Dhariwal, Arvind Neelakantan, Pranav Shyam, Girish Sastry, Amanda Askell, Sandhini Agarwal, Ariel Herbert-Voss, Gretchen Krueger, Tom Henighan, Rewon Child, Aditya Ramesh, Daniel Ziegler, Jeffrey Wu, Clemens Winter, Chris Hesse, Mark Chen, Eric Sigler, Mateusz Litwin, Scott Gray, Benjamin Chess, Jack Clark, Christopher Berner, Sam McCandlish, Alec Radford, Ilya Sutskever, and Dario Amodei. 2020. Language models are few-shot learners. In *Advances in Neural Information Processing Systems*, volume 33, pages 1877–1901. Curran Associates, Inc.

Lili Chen, Kevin Lu, Aravind Rajeswaran, Kimin Lee, Aditya Grover, Michael Laskin, Pieter Abbeel, Aravind Srinivas, and Igor Mordatch. 2021. Decision transformer: Reinforcement learning via sequence modeling. In *Advances in Neural Information Processing Systems*.

Kyunghyun Cho, Bart van Merriënboer, Dzmitry Bahdanau, and Yoshua Bengio. 2014. On the properties of neural machine translation: Encoder–decoder approaches. In *Proceedings of SSST-8, Eighth Workshop on Syntax, Semantics and Structure in Statistical Translation*, pages 103–111.

Marc-Alexandre Côté, Ákos Kádár, Xingdi Yuan, Ben Kybartas, Tavian Barnes, Emery Fine, James Moore, Matthew Hausknecht, Layla El Asri, Mahmoud Adada, et al. 2018. Textworld: A learning environment for text-based games. In *Workshop on Computer Games*, pages 41–75. Springer.

Jacob Devlin, Ming-Wei Chang, Kenton Lee, and Kristina Toutanova. 2019. BERT: Pre-training of deep bidirectional transformers for language understanding. In *Proceedings of the 2019 Conference of the North American Chapter of the Association for Computational Linguistics: Human Language Technologies, Volume 1 (Long and Short Papers)*, pages 4171–4186, Minneapolis, Minnesota. Association for Computational Linguistics.

Michael P Georgeff and Amy L Lansky. 1986. Procedural knowledge. *Proceedings of the IEEE*, 74(10):1383–1398.

Daniel Gordon, Aniruddha Kembhavi, Mohammad Rastegari, Joseph Redmon, Dieter Fox, and Ali Farhadi. 2018. Iqa: Visual question answering in interactive environments. In *Proceedings of the IEEE Conference on Computer Vision and Pattern Recognition*, pages 4089–4098.

Matteo Hessel, Joseph Modayil, Hado Van Hasselt, Tom Schaul, Georg Ostrovski, Will Dabney, Dan Horgan, Bilal Piot, Mohammad Azar, and David Silver. 2018. Rainbow: Combining improvements in deep reinforcement learning. In *Thirty-second AAAI conference on artificial intelligence*.

Michael Janner, Qiyang Li, and Sergey Levine. 2021. Offline reinforcement learning as one big sequence modeling problem. In *Advances in Neural Information Processing Systems*.

Diederik P. Kingma and Jimmy Ba. 2015. Adam: A method for stochastic optimization. In *ICLR (Poster)*.

Jieh-Sheng Lee and Jieh Hsiang. 2019. Patentbert: Patent classification with fine-tuning a pre-trained bert model. *arXiv preprint arXiv:1906.02124*.

Manuel Mager, Ramón Fernandez Astudillo, Tahira Naseem, Md Arafat Sultan, Young-Suk Lee, Radu Florian, and Salim Roukos. 2020. GPT-too: A language-model-first approach for AMR-to-text generation. In *Proceedings of the 58th Annual Meeting of the Association for Computational Linguistics*, pages 1846–1852, Online. Association for Computational Linguistics.

Volodymyr Mnih, Koray Kavukcuoglu, David Silver, Andrei A. Rusu, Joel Veness, Marc G. Bellemare, Alex Graves, Martin Riedmiller, Andreas K. Fidjeland, Georg Ostrovski, Stig Petersen, Charles Beattie, Amir Sadik, Ioannis Antonoglou, Helen King, Dharshan Kumaran, Daan Wierstra, Shane Legg, and Demis Hassabis. 2015. Human-level control through deep reinforcement learning. *Nature*, 518(7540):529–533.

Alec Radford, Jeffrey Wu, Rewon Child, David Luan, Dario Amodei, Ilya Sutskever, et al. 2019. Language models are unsupervised multitask learners. *OpenAI blog*, 1(8):9.

Aditya Ramesh, Mikhail Pavlov, Gabriel Goh, Scott Gray, Chelsea Voss, Alec Radford, Mark Chen, and Ilya Sutskever. 2021. Zero-shot text-to-image generation. In *Proceedings of the 38th International Conference on Machine Learning*, volume 139 of *Proceedings of Machine Learning Research*, pages 8821–8831. PMLR.

Adam Trischler, Tong Wang, Xingdi Yuan, Justin Harris, Alessandro Sordoni, Philip Bachman, and Kaheer Suleman. 2017. NewsQA: A machine comprehension dataset. In *Proceedings of the 2nd Workshop on Representation Learning for NLP*, pages 191–200, Vancouver, Canada. Association for Computational Linguistics.

Hado Van Hasselt, Arthur Guez, and David Silver. 2016. Deep reinforcement learning with double q-learning. In *Proceedings of the AAAI conference on artificial intelligence*, volume 30.

Ashish Vaswani, Noam Shazeer, Niki Parmar, Jakob Uszkoreit, Llion Jones, Aidan N Gomez, Łukasz Kaiser, and Illia Polosukhin. 2017. Attention is all you need. In *Advances in neural information processing systems*, pages 5998–6008.

Xingdi Yuan, Marc-Alexandre Côté, Jie Fu, Zhouhan Lin, Chris Pal, Yoshua Bengio, and Adam Trischler.

2019. Interactive language learning by question answering. In *Proceedings of the 2019 Conference on Empirical Methods in Natural Language Processing and the 9th International Joint Conference on Natural Language Processing (EMNLP-IJCNLP)*, pages 2796–2813, Hong Kong, China. Association for Computational Linguistics.

Xingdi Yuan, Marc-Alexandre Côté, Alessandro Sordoni, Romain Laroche, Remi Tachet des Combes, Matthew J. Hausknecht, and Adam Trischler. 2018. Counting to explore and generalize in text-based games. *CoRR*, abs/1806.11525.

Sina Zarrieß, Henrik Voigt, and Simeon Schüz. 2021. Decoding methods in neural language generation: A survey. *Information*, 12(9).

A Hyperparameter Tuning

Hyperparameters of the DT and BERT are given in Table 4.

	DT	BERT
Hyperparameters	**Value**	
Number of layers	2	12
Number of attention heads	8	12
Embedding dimension	256	768
Batch size	128	12
State context window tokens	180	512
Context length (K)	50	-
Max Epochs	2000	30
Dropout	0.5	0.1
Learning rate	1×10^{-4}	1×10^{-5}
Adam betas	(0.9, 0.95)	
Grad norm clip	0.25	
Weight decay	0.1	

Table 4: Decision Transformer and the BERT QA hyperparameters. For the DT, Context length K refers to the amount of previous time steps with which the Transformer can conditiona on. Context State context window refers to the number of tokens from the state to be used for prediction. Adam (Kingma and Ba, 2015) is used as optimiser in conjunction with the specified learning rate, linear warmup and cosine weight decay.

A.1 Decision Transformer

A.1.1 Location

As can be seen in Table 5, the sufficient information score peaking at $R_1 = 2$ indicates optimal state-space exploration for location questions when the potential for future reward is moderate for random and fixed map types. While the QA accuracy was highest for both settings when the initial reward was the maximum of the training set, we opted to test the DT's question answering and information gathering capabilities at $R_1 = 2$ as this yielded the highest combined sufficient information and QA accuracy score.

A.1.2 Existence

Using both sufficient information and QA accuracy, the optimal initial reward for fixed map existence questions was determined to be 4.0, with the DT achieving a QA accuracy of 0.660 and a sufficient information score of 0.263 on the validation set. In random map settings, the DT scored a validation accuracy of 0.720 with a corresponding sufficient information score of 0.298, where the initial reward was determined to be the maximum of the training set 3.94.

A.1.3 Attribute

The best sufficient information and QA accuracy combinations for the Decision Transformer were achieved at an initial reward of 2.0 for fixed and 5.0 for random map types. On the validation set, the fixed map DT achieved a QA accuracy of 0.533 and a SI score of 0.056. Random map saw a similar SI of 0.057 but worse QA accuracy of 0.460.

A.2 BERT Model

A.2.1 Location

Based on data gathered using the online-evaluation dataset, the optimal initial return-to-go for location type questions was 2.0. Using the BERT model for QA yielded an accuracy of 0.227 for fixed maps and 0.393 for random maps. The BERT model achieved a higher QA accuracy than sufficient information score during evaluation, indicating that the context window spanning multiple states was a boon to QA accuracy. During training, the BERT model achieved almost perfect scores for question-answering on the held-out set of offline trajectories, seen in Table 3.

A.2.2 Existence

Using the online-validation set, we determined optimal starting reward values of 3.0 for fixed map and 3.94 for random. These values were associated with a QA accuracy of 0.64 for fixed and 0.647 for random map types. However, scores were significantly lower than the offline validation set used during training, where QA accuracy of 0.778 and 0.779 was achieved for fixed and random maps, respectively.

A.2.3 Attribute

In the offline validation set, the BERT model scored a QA accuracy of 0.616 for random and 0.780 for fixed map settings. On the online validation set, we observed the maximum combination of QA and sufficient information for the BERT model at an R_1 of 3.0 for fixed and 2.0 for random where the BERT QA model had an accuracy of 0.507 and 0.660 for random and fixed map types, respectively. However, we opted to use the maximum of the train set 4.03 when evaluating on the test set for random map types. This is due to the BERT QA model having a high standard deviation of 0.156 and an average QA accuracy of 0.640, indicating greater potential for high QA accuracy. Moreover, the sufficient information score associated with this accuracy is 0.056 - higher than the random map with an initial reward of 2.0.

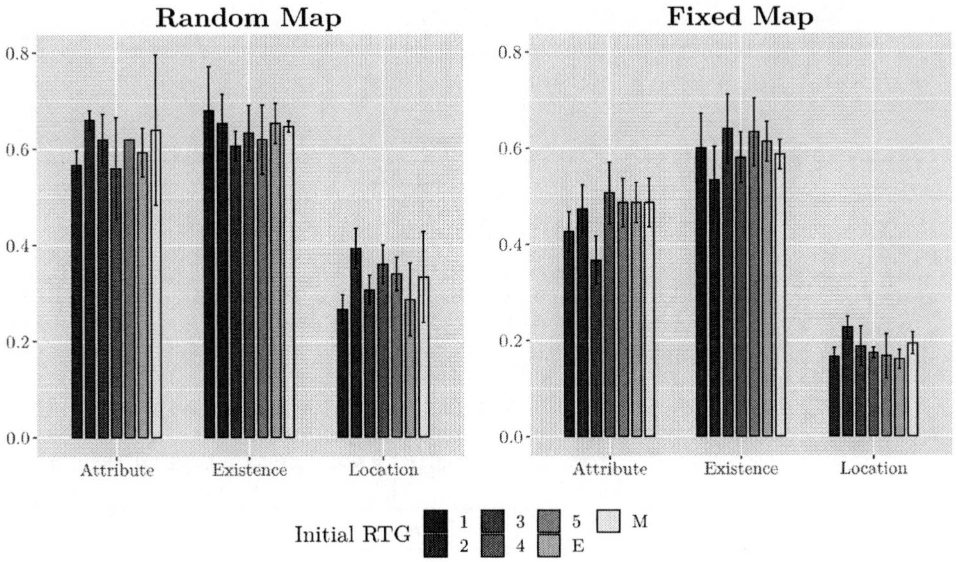

Figure 3: Barplot showing QA accuracy of the BERT QA model on the validation set when trained in the 500 games setting with different initial returns-to-go (RTG). See results in Table 5.

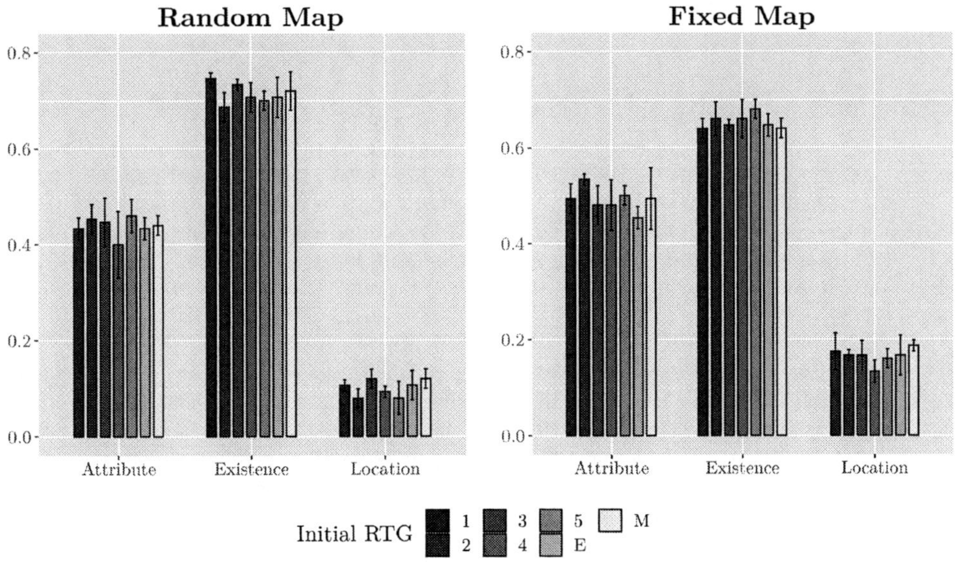

Figure 4: Barplot showing QA accuracy of the Decision Transformer's answer-prediction head on the validation set when trained in the 500 games setting with different initial returns-to-go (RTG). See results in Table 5.

	Question Type					
	Attribute					
	Fixed			**Random**		
Initial RTG	**BERT**	**DT**	**SI**	**BERT**	**DT**	**SI**
1	0.427 ± 0.0416	0.493 ± 0.0306	0.052 ± 0.0135	0.567 ± 0.0306	0.433 ± 0.0231	0.050 ± 0.0083
2	0.473 ± 0.0503	**0.533 ± 0.0115**	**0.056 ± 0.0094**	**0.660 ± 0.0200**	0.453 ± 0.0306	**0.048 ± 0.0039**
3	0.367 ± 0.0503	0.480 ± 0.0400	0.051 ± 0.0043	0.620 ± 0.0529	0.447 ± 0.0503	0.054 ± 0.0034
4	**0.507 ± 0.0643**	0.480 ± 0.0529	**0.056 ± 0.0058**	0.560 ± 0.1058	0.400 ± 0.0693	0.054 ± 0.0014
5	0.487 ± 0.0503	0.500 ± 0.0200	0.056 ± 0.0007	0.620 ± 0.0000	**0.460 ± 0.0346**	**0.057 ± 0.0033**
Sampling	0.487 ± 0.0416	0.453 ± 0.0231	0.051 ± 0.0050	0.593 ± 0.0503	0.433 ± 0.0231	0.052 ± 0.0097
Max	0.487 ± 0.0503	0.493 ± 0.0643	0.055 ± 0.0021	**0.640 ± 0.1562**	0.440 ± 0.0200	**0.056 ± 0.0020**
	Existence					
	Fixed			**Random**		
Initial RTG	**BERT**	**DT**	**SI**	**BERT**	**DT**	**SI**
1	0.600 ± 0.0721	0.640 ± 0.0200	0.216 ± 0.0314	0.680 ± 0.0917	0.747 ± 0.0115	0.200 ± 0.0416
2	0.533 ± 0.0702	0.660 ± 0.0346	0.259 ± 0.0051	0.653 ± 0.0611	0.687 ± 0.0306	0.277 ± 0.0441
3	**0.640 ± 0.0721**	0.647 ± 0.0115	**0.265 ± 0.0161**	0.607 ± 0.0306	0.733 ± 0.0115	0.269 ± 0.0075
4	0.580 ± 0.0529	**0.660 ± 0.0400**	**0.263 ± 0.0180**	0.633 ± 0.0577	0.707 ± 0.0306	0.291 ± 0.0476
5	0.633 ± 0.0702	0.680 ± 0.0200	0.222 ± 0.0166	0.620 ± 0.0721	0.700 ± 0.0200	0.310 ± 0.0205
Sampling	0.613 ± 0.0416	0.647 ± 0.0231	0.180 ± 0.0467	0.653 ± 0.0416	0.707 ± 0.0416	0.250 ± 0.0070
Max	0.587 ± 0.0306	0.640 ± 0.0200	0.270 ± 0.0409	**0.647 ± 0.0115**	**0.720 ± 0.0400**	**0.298 ± 0.0302**
	Location					
	Fixed			**Random**		
Initial RTG	**BERT**	**DT**	**SI**	**BERT**	**DT**	**SI**
1	0.165 ± 0.0191	0.175 ± 0.0379	0.165 ± 0.0191	0.267 ± 0.0306	0.107 ± 0.0115	0.267 ± 0.0306
2	**0.227 ± 0.0231**	**0.167 ± 0.0115**	**0.233 ± 0.0115**	**0.393 ± 0.0416**	**0.080 ± 0.0200**	**0.387 ± 0.0503**
3	0.187 ± 0.0416	0.167 ± 0.0306	0.187 ± 0.0416	0.307 ± 0.0306	0.120 ± 0.0200	0.307 ± 0.0306
4	0.173 ± 0.0115	0.133 ± 0.0231	0.173 ± 0.0115	0.360 ± 0.0400	0.093 ± 0.0115	0.347 ± 0.0306
5	0.167 ± 0.0462	0.160 ± 0.0200	0.167 ± 0.0462	0.340 ± 0.0346	0.080 ± 0.0346	0.333 ± 0.0306
Sampling	0.160 ± 0.0200	0.167 ± 0.0416	0.167 ± 0.0115	0.287 ± 0.0757	0.107 ± 0.0306	0.287 ± 0.0757
Max	0.193 ± 0.0231	0.187 ± 0.0115	0.193 ± 0.0231	0.333 ± 0.0945	0.120 ± 0.0200	0.327 ± 0.0702

Table 5: Question-answering accuracy of the BERT model's and the Decision Transformer's answer prediction head as well as the Decision Transformer's average sufficient information (SI) score on validation set at different initial return-to-go (RTG) values. Bold values indicate the combined highest QA and sufficient information score with the associated initial RTG value also bolded. *Sampling* indicates R_1 was randomly sampled from an exponential distribution. *Max* represents the maximum of the training set for that experiment configuration (see Table 1). Summary statistics were calculated over 4 seeds - see code implementation for details.

Question Type						
Attribute						
	Fixed			**Random**		
Initial RTG	**BERT-10K**	**DT-10K**	**SI**	**BERT-10K**	**DT-10K**	**SI**
1	0.515 ± 0.0719	**0.590 ± 0.0258**	0.054 ± 0.0074	0.490 ± 0.0529	0.410 ± 0.0258	0.053 ± 0.0123
2	0.485 ± 0.0342	0.580 ± 0.0542	0.051 ± 0.0094	**0.510 ± 0.1013**	0.410 ± 0.0115	0.044 ± 0.0061
3	0.450 ± 0.0600	0.550 ± 0.0258	0.055 ± 0.0023	0.450 ± 0.0416	0.420 ± 0.0432	0.047 ± 0.0082
4	0.440 ± 0.0163	0.580 ± 0.0365	0.056 ± 0.0040	0.430 ± 0.0775	**0.445 ± 0.0191**	0.051 ± 0.0071
5	**0.525 ± 0.0526**	0.560 ± 0.0163	0.055 ± 0.0019	0.470 ± 0.0825	0.410 ± 0.0200	0.050 ± 0.0026
Sampling	0.455 ± 0.0681	0.545 ± 0.0300	0.052 ± 0.0100	0.490 ± 0.0200	0.415 ± 0.0100	0.044 ± 0.0042
Max	0.420 ± 0.0283	0.560 ± 0.0163	0.051 ± 0.0052	0.470 ± 0.0476	0.410 ± 0.0383	0.054 ± 0.0102
Existence						
	Fixed			**Random**		
Initial RTG	**BERT-10K**	**DT-10K**	**SI**	**BERT-10K**	**DT-10K**	**SI**
1	0.595 ± 0.0574	0.590 ± 0.0258	0.165 ± 0.0148	0.740 ± 0.0400	0.705 ± 0.0300	0.165 ± 0.0143
2	0.575 ± 0.0412	0.625 ± 0.0252	0.195 ± 0.0256	0.640 ± 0.0566	0.680 ± 0.0283	0.219 ± 0.0318
3	0.610 ± 0.0258	0.645 ± 0.0342	0.232 ± 0.0235	0.620 ± 0.1007	0.690 ± 0.0600	0.233 ± 0.0303
4	**0.650 ± 0.0346**	0.640 ± 0.0365	0.251 ± 0.0538	**0.685 ± 0.0252**	0.670 ± 0.0346	0.240 ± 0.0175
5	0.560 ± 0.0283	**0.690 ± 0.0663**	0.286 ± 0.0421	0.645 ± 0.0661	**0.685 ± 0.0473**	0.253 ± 0.0362
Sampling	0.645 ± 0.0551	0.655 ± 0.0300	0.214 ± 0.0305	0.660 ± 0.0283	0.725 ± 0.0252	0.179 ± 0.0372
Max	0.635 ± 0.0823	0.630 ± 0.0702	0.229 ± 0.0471	0.630 ± 0.0577	0.675 ± 0.0379	0.243 ± 0.0328
Location						
	Fixed			**Random**		
Initial RTG	**BERT-10K**	**DT-10K**	**SI**	**BERT-10K**	**DT-10K**	**SI**
1	0.150 ± 0.0346	0.130 ± 0.0115	0.195 ± 0.0300	0.130 ± 0.0258	**0.130 ± 0.0115**	0.170 ± 0.0476
2	0.135 ± 0.0342	0.155 ± 0.0500	0.190 ± 0.0115	0.130 ± 0.0258	0.105 ± 0.0300	0.165 ± 0.0100
3	0.155 ± 0.0300	0.150 ± 0.0383	0.220 ± 0.0432	0.155 ± 0.0526	0.105 ± 0.0342	0.135 ± 0.0300
4	0.135 ± 0.0500	0.130 ± 0.0258	0.230 ± 0.0200	0.145 ± 0.0300	0.120 ± 0.0432	0.150 ± 0.0346
5	0.135 ± 0.0300	0.135 ± 0.0473	0.230 ± 0.0258	**0.160 ± 0.0432**	0.110 ± 0.0383	0.170 ± 0.0200
Sampling	0.150 ± 0.0383	0.145 ± 0.0100	0.180 ± 0.0163	0.125 ± 0.0412	0.105 ± 0.0100	0.160 ± 0.0163
Max	**0.145 ± 0.0252**	**0.150 ± 0.0115**	0.240 ± 0.0327	0.145 ± 0.0300	0.120 ± 0.0432	0.150 ± 0.0346

Table 6: Question-answering accuracy of the 10K variation BERT model's and Decision Transformer's answer prediction head as well as the Decision Transformer's average sufficient information (SI) score on validation set at different initial return-to-go (RTG) values. Bold values indicate the combined highest QA and sufficient information score with the associated initial RTG value also bolded. Both models were trained on only 10 thousand episodes of data.

Model	Location		Existence		Attribute	
	Fixed					
	Train	**Test**	**Train**	**Test**	**Train**	**Test**
Random	-	0.027	-	0.497	-	0.496
	500 games					
DQN	0.430 (0.430)	0.224 (0.244)	0.742 (0.136)	0.674 (0.279)	0.700 (0.015)	0.534 (0.014)
DDQN	0.406 (0.406)	0.218 (0.228)	0.734 (0.173)	0.626 (0.213)	0.714 (0.021)	0.508 (0.026)
Rainbow	0.358 (0.358)	0.190 (0.196)	0.768 (0.187)	0.656 (0.207)	0.736 (0.032)	0.496 (0.029)
DT	-	0.168 (0.232)	-	0.668 (0.254)	-	0.504 (0.057)
DT-BERT	-	**0.232 (0.232)**	-	0.626 (0.258)	-	0.524 (0.058)
DT - 10K	-	0.146 (0.302)	-	**0.688 (0.240)**	-	0.488 (0.058)
DT-BERT - 10K	-	0.124 (0.302)	-	0.612 (0.241)	-	**0.552 (0.060)**

Table 7: Results of Fixed Map Experiments

Model	Location		Existence		Attribute	
	Random					
	Train	**Test**	**Train**	**Test**	**Train**	**Test**
Random	-	0.034	-	0.5	-	0.499
	500 games					
DQN	0.430 (0.430)	0.204 (0.216)	0.752 (0.162)	0.678 (0.214)	0.678 (0.019)	0.530 (0.017)
DDQN	0.458 (0.458)	0.222 (0.246)	0.754 (0.158)	0.656 (0.188)	0.716 (0.024)	0.486 (0.023)
Rainbow	0.370 (0.370)	0.172 (0.178)	0.748 (0.275)	0.678 (0.191)	0.636 (0.020)	0.494 (0.017)
DT	-	0.104 (0.264)	-	**0.722 (0.277)**	-	0.526 (0.058)
DT-BERT	-	**0.270 (0.264)**	-	0.654 (0.277)	-	**0.538 (0.060)**
DT - 10K	-	0.102 (0.220)	-	0.618 (0.255)	-	0.490 (0.048)
DT-BERT - 10K	-	0.076 (0.204)	-	0.676 (0.223)	-	0.518 (0.049)

Table 8: Results of Random Map Experiments

Automatic Exploration of Textual Environments with Language-Conditioned Autotelic Agents

Laetitia Teodorescu
Inria
laetitia.teodorescu@inria.fr

Xingdi Yuan
Microsoft Research
eric.yuan@microsoft.com

Marc-Alexandre Côté
Microsoft Research
macote@microsoft.com

Pierre-Yves Oudeyer
Inria
pierre-yves.oudeyer@inria.fr

This extended abstract discusses the opportunities and challenges of studying intrinsically-motivated agents for exploration in textual environments.

Humans begin their life with very few skills, and over the course of only a few years learn complex motor coordination and locomotion capabilities, begin mastering vocalization and language, and form a rich model of their physical and social surroundings. One of the main drivers of this phenomenal knowledge acquisition is intrinsically-motivated exploration (Oudeyer and Kaplan, 2007), for instance through exploratory play (Chu and Schulz, 2020; Davidson et al., 2022). The developmental perspective on AI tries to emulate this exploratory behavior in artificial agents to achieve mastery of diverse and complex repertoires of skills (Forestier et al., 2017). When placed in open-ended environments, a successful intrinsically motivated agent will explore the space of interesting and diverse outcomes, ignoring random and unachievable subspaces of the world, reusing its previously acquired skills as stepping stones (Stanley and Lehman, 2015) to discover new ones.

One possible implementation of exploration in RL agents are so-called autotelic agents (Colas, 2021), that is, goal-conditioned Reinforcement Learning (RL) agents operating in rewardless environments that are able to choose what goal to pursue. In this case, the reward is given by a goal-satisfaction function and not extrinsically by the environment. Goal-conditioned policies have been extensively studied in the case of extrinsic goals (Schaul et al., 2015). In the case of intrinsically chosen goals, the goal-selection mechanism allows autotelic agents to form a self-curriculum, progressing from easier to increasingly harder goals until all achievable skills have been mastered. In this perspective, the goal representation is of paramount importance. Most previous works (for instance Andrychowicz et al. (2017)) have used concrete end-state representations such as raw observations, images or embeddings, which has some drawbacks. A goal should be insensitive to changes in the environment that are uncontrollable (such as the color of the sky), to avoid the agent targeting impossible goals (for instance changing the sky color), or to provide useful abstraction for goal achievement (such as considering the goal of navigating to the garden is satisfied regardless of sky color). Furthermore, the agent should ideally be able to combine known goals into novel ones. **Goals expressed as language** (Tam et al., 2022; Colas et al., 2020; Mu et al., 2022) fulfill both conditions: they are at once abstract and combinatorial (Szabó, 2020); they are thus a prime way for autotelic agents to self-specify goals to be executed in the environment.

1 A bridge between autotelic agents and text environments

The main point of this essay is the relevance of studying language autotelic agents in textual environments (Côté et al., 2018; Hausknecht et al., 2020; Wang et al., 2022), both for testing exploration methods in a context that is at once simple experimentally and rich from the perspective of environment interactions; and for transferring the skills of general-purpose agents trained to explore in an autonomous way to the predefined tasks of textual environment benchmarks. We identify three key properties, plus one additional benefit, of text worlds:

1. Depth of learnable skills: skills learnable in the world should involve multiple low-level actions and be nested, such that mastering one skill opens up the possibility of mastering more complex skills. Interactive fiction (IF) (Hausknecht et al., 2020) games usually feature an entire narrative and extensive maps, such that navigating and passing obstacles requires many successful actions (and subgoals) to be completed. While the origi-

Proceedings of the 3rd Wordplay: When Language Meets Games Workshop (Wordplay 2022), pages 59 - 62
July 14, 2022 ©2022 Association for Computational Linguistics

nal TextWorld levels were not as deep as would be desirable, other non-IF text worlds such as ScienceWorld feature nested repertoires of skills (such as learning to navigate to learn to grow plants to learn the rules of Mendelian genomics);

2. Breadth of the world: there should be many paths to explore in the environment; this ensures that we train agents that are able to follow a wide diversity of possible goals, instead of learning to achieve goals along a linear path. This allows us to study generally-capable agents. Some IF games are very linear, having a clear progression from start to finish (e.g., Acorn Court, Detective; others have huge maps that an agent has to explore before it can progress in the quest (e.g., Zork, Hitchhiker's Guide to the Galaxy). Exploration heuristics are a part of some successful methods for playing IF with RL (Yao et al., 2020). ScienceWorld (Wang et al., 2022) has an underlying physical engine allowing for a combinatorial explosion of possibilities like making new objects, combining existing objects, changing states of matter, etc.

3. Niches of progress: real-world environments have both easy skills and unlearnable skills. Our simulated environments should mimic this property to test the agent's ability to focus only on highly learnable parts of the space and avoid spending effort on uncontrollable aspects of the environment. In textual environments, high depth implies that some skills are much more learnable than others, already implementing some progress niches. The combinatorial property of language goals allows us to define many unfeasible goals, goals that an autotelic agent has to avoid spending too many resources on.

4. Language representation for goals: a language-conditioned agent has to learn to ground its goal representation in its environment (Harnad, 1990; Hill et al., 2020), to know when a given observation or sequence of observations satisfies a given goal, or to know what goals were achieved in a given trajectory. This grounding is made much simpler in environments with a single modality; relating language goals to language observations is simpler than grounding language in pixels or image embeddings. This allows us to study language-based exploration in a simpler context.

2 Drivers of exploration in autotelic agents

We identify three main drivers of exploration in autotelic agents. Environments we use should support exploration algorithms that implement these principles; the resulting agents then have a chance to acquire a diverse set of skills that can be repurposed for solving the benchmarks proposed by textual environments.

1. Goal self-curriculum: automatic goal selection (Portelas et al., 2020) allows the agent to refine its skills on the edge of what it currently masters. Among metrics used to select goals are novelty/surprise of a goal (Tam et al., 2022; Burda et al., 2018), intermediate competence on goals (Campero et al., 2020), ensemble disagreement (Pathak et al., 2019), or (absolute) learning progress (Colas et al., 2019). Progress niches in textual environments support such goal curriculum;

2. Additional exploration after goal achievement: after achieving a given goal, the agent continue to run for a time to push the boundary of explored space (Ecoffet et al., 2021). The depth of text worlds makes goal chaining relevant, such that an agent that has achieved a known goal can imagine additional goals to pursue. Random exploration can also be used once a known goal has been achieved. Agents exploring in textual environments and choosing uniformly among the set of valid actions in a given state have a high chance of effecting meaningful changes in the environment, making discovery of new skills probable. This property is relevant in any environment with high depth, and both IF and ScienceWorld fit this description.

3. Goal composition: as mentioned above, this means using the compositionality afforded by language goals to imagine novel goals in the environment (Colas et al., 2020). Goal-chaining is an example of composition, but language offers many other composition possibilities, such as recombining known verbs, nouns and attributes in novel ways, or making analogies. This is relevant if there exists some transfer between the skills required to accomplish similar goal constructions (e.g., picking up an apple and picking up a carrot requires very similar actions if both are in the kitchen). This is at least partially true in textual environments where objects of the same type usually have similar affordances.

3 Challenges for autotelic textual agents

Text worlds bring a set of unique challenges for autotelic agents, among which we foresee:

1. The goal space can be very large. An agent with a limited training budget needs to focus on a subset of the goal space, possibly discovering only a fraction of what is discoverable within the environment. This calls for finer goal-sampling approaches that encourage the agent at making the most out of its allocated time to explore the environment. In addition, we need better methods to push the agent's exploration towards certain parts of the space (e.g., warm-starting the replay buffer with existing trajectories, providing linguistic commonsense knowledge);

2. The action space is also very large in textual environments, making exploration (especially methods based on random action selection) potentially challenging.

3. Agents must be trajectory-efficient for a given goal; complex goals might be seen only once;

4. Catastrophic forgetting needs to be alleviated, so that learning to achieve new goals does not impair the skills learned previously;

5. Partial observability means that agent architectures need to include some form of memory.

Agents trained in such environments will learn a form of language use, not by predicting the most likely sequence of words from a large-scale dataset (Radford and Narasimhan, 2018; Brown et al., 2020) but by learning to use it pragmatically to effect changes in the environment. Of course, the limits of the autotelic agent's world will mean the limits of its language; an interesting development is to build agents that explore textual environments to refine external linguistic knowledge provided by a pretrained language model. This external knowledge repository can be seen as culturally-accumulated common sense, a perspective that is related to so-called Vygotskian AI (Colas, 2021) in which a developmental agent learns by interacting with an external social partner that imparts outside language knowledge and organizes the world so as to facilitate the autotelic agent's exploration.

To conclude, textual environments are ideal testbeds for autotelic language-conditioned agents, and conversely such agents can bring progress on text world benchmarks. There is also promise in the interaction between exploratory agents and large language models encoding exterior linguistic knowledge. Preliminary steps have been taken in this direction (Madotto et al., 2020) but the full breadth of drivers of exploration we identify has yet to be studied. We hope to foster discussion, define concrete implementations and identify challenges by bringing together the developmental perspective on AI and the textual environment community.

References

Marcin Andrychowicz, Filip Wolski, Alex Ray, Jonas Schneider, Rachel Fong, Peter Welinder, Bob McGrew, Josh Tobin, OpenAI Pieter Abbeel, and Wojciech Zaremba. 2017. Hindsight experience replay. *Advances in neural information processing systems*, 30.

Tom Brown, Benjamin Mann, Nick Ryder, Melanie Subbiah, Jared D Kaplan, Prafulla Dhariwal, Arvind Neelakantan, Pranav Shyam, Girish Sastry, Amanda Askell, et al. 2020. Language models are few-shot learners. *Advances in neural information processing systems*, 33:1877–1901.

Yuri Burda, Harrison Edwards, Amos Storkey, and Oleg Klimov. 2018. Exploration by random network distillation. *arXiv preprint arXiv:1810.12894*.

Andres Campero, Roberta Raileanu, Heinrich Küttler, Joshua B Tenenbaum, Tim Rocktäschel, and Edward Grefenstette. 2020. Learning with amigo: Adversarially motivated intrinsic goals. *arXiv preprint arXiv:2006.12122*.

Junyi Chu and Laura Schulz. 2020. Play, curiosity, and cognition. *Annual Review of Developmental Psychology*, 2.

Cédric Colas. 2021. *Towards Vygotskian Autotelic Agents : Learning Skills with Goals, Language and Intrinsically Motivated Deep Reinforcement Learning*. Theses, Université de Bordeaux.

Cédric Colas, Pierre Fournier, Mohamed Chetouani, Olivier Sigaud, and Pierre-Yves Oudeyer. 2019. Curious: intrinsically motivated modular multi-goal reinforcement learning. In *International conference on machine learning*, pages 1331–1340. PMLR.

Cédric Colas, Tristan Karch, Nicolas Lair, Jean-Michel Dussoux, Clément Moulin-Frier, Peter Dominey, and Pierre-Yves Oudeyer. 2020. Language as a cognitive tool to imagine goals in curiosity driven exploration. *Advances in Neural Information Processing Systems*, 33:3761–3774.

Marc-Alexandre Côté, Akos Kádár, Xingdi Yuan, Ben Kybartas, Tavian Barnes, Emery Fine, James Moore, Matthew Hausknecht, Layla El Asri, Mahmoud Adada, et al. 2018. Textworld: A learning environment for text-based games. In *Workshop on Computer Games*, pages 41–75. Springer.

Guy Davidson, Todd M Gureckis, and Brenden M Lake. 2022. Creativity, compositionality, and common sense in human goal generation.

Adrien Ecoffet, Joost Huizinga, Joel Lehman, Kenneth O Stanley, and Jeff Clune. 2021. First return, then explore. *Nature*, 590(7847):580–586.

Sébastien Forestier, Rémy Portelas, Yoan Mollard, and Pierre-Yves Oudeyer. 2017. Intrinsically motivated goal exploration processes with automatic curriculum learning. *arXiv preprint arXiv:1708.02190*.

Stevan Harnad. 1990. The symbol grounding problem. *Physica D: Nonlinear Phenomena*, 42(1-3):335–346.

Matthew Hausknecht, Prithviraj Ammanabrolu, Marc-Alexandre Côté, and Xingdi Yuan. 2020. Interactive fiction games: A colossal adventure. In *Proceedings of the AAAI Conference on Artificial Intelligence*, volume 34, pages 7903–7910.

Felix Hill, Olivier Tieleman, Tamara von Glehn, Nathaniel Wong, Hamza Merzic, and Stephen Clark. 2020. Grounded language learning fast and slow. *arXiv preprint arXiv:2009.01719*.

Andrea Madotto, Mahdi Namazifar, Joost Huizinga, Piero Molino, Adrien Ecoffet, Huaixiu Zheng, Alexandros Papangelis, Dian Yu, Chandra Khatri, and Gokhan Tur. 2020. Exploration based language learning for text-based games. *arXiv preprint arXiv:2001.08868*.

Jesse Mu, Victor Zhong, Roberta Raileanu, Minqi Jiang, Noah Goodman, Tim Rocktäschel, and Edward Grefenstette. 2022. Improving intrinsic exploration with language abstractions. *arXiv preprint arXiv:2202.08938*.

Pierre-Yves Oudeyer and Frederic Kaplan. 2007. What is intrinsic motivation? a typology of computational approaches. *Frontiers in neurorobotics*, 1:6–6. 18958277[pmid].

Deepak Pathak, Dhiraj Gandhi, and Abhinav Gupta. 2019. Self-supervised exploration via disagreement. In *International conference on machine learning*, pages 5062–5071. PMLR.

Rémy Portelas, Cédric Colas, Lilian Weng, Katja Hofmann, and Pierre-Yves Oudeyer. 2020. Automatic curriculum learning for deep rl: A short survey. *arXiv preprint arXiv:2003.04664*.

Alec Radford and Karthik Narasimhan. 2018. Improving language understanding by generative pretraining.

Tom Schaul, Dan Horgan, Karol Gregor, and David Silver. 2015. Universal value function approximators. page 1312–1320.

Kenneth O. Stanley and Joel Lehman. 2015. *Why Greatness Cannot Be Planned: The Myth of the Objective*. Springer Publishing Company, Incorporated.

Zoltán Gendler Szabó. 2020. Compositionality. In Edward N. Zalta, editor, *The Stanford Encyclopedia of Philosophy*, Fall 2020 edition. Metaphysics Research Lab, Stanford University.

Allison C Tam, Neil C Rabinowitz, Andrew K Lampinen, Nicholas A Roy, Stephanie CY Chan, DJ Strouse, Jane X Wang, Andrea Banino, and Felix Hill. 2022. Semantic exploration from language abstractions and pretrained representations. *arXiv preprint arXiv:2204.05080*.

Ruoyao Wang, Peter Jansen, Marc-Alexandre Côté, and Prithviraj Ammanabrolu. 2022. Scienceworld: Is your agent smarter than a 5th grader? *arXiv preprint arXiv:2203.07540*.

Shunyu Yao, Rohan Rao, Matthew Hausknecht, and Karthik Narasimhan. 2020. Keep calm and explore: Language models for action generation in text-based games. *arXiv preprint arXiv:2010.02903*.

Author Index